FOCUS ON ARCHITECTURE AND SCULPTURE

By the same author

NEW PHOTO VISION

JULIA MARGARET CAMERON

THE MAN BEHIND THE CAMERA

LEWIS CARROLL — PHOTOGRAPHER

FOCUS ON
ARCHITECTURE AND SCULPTURE

AN ORIGINAL APPROACH TO THE PHOTOGRAPHY
OF ARCHITECTURE AND SCULPTURE

BY HELMUT GERNSHEIM
Fellow of the Royal Photographic Society

With a Foreword by Nikolaus Pevsner
Joint Editor of the Architectural Review

LONDON
THE FOUNTAIN PRESS

First Published November 1949

Printed in Great Britain
Text by Chorley & Pickersgill Ltd Leeds
Plates by Maxwell Love & Co Ltd London
Blocks bv The Arc Engraving Co Ltd London
Binding by The Garden City Press Ltd Letchworth

ACKNOWLEDGMENTS

MY MAIN debt is to Dr R. Wittkower of the Warburg Institute, whose advice and suggestions, and often active help when no other assistance was procurable, proved invaluable.

Further, I wish to express my gratitude to Dr N. Pevsner of the *Architectural Review*, who greatly encouraged me in my work and first drew public attention to it, and to Sir Kenneth and Lady Clark, through whose kind interest I was privileged to arrange a number of exhibitions at the Churchill Club. My thanks are also due to my wife for the large amount of work which fell to her share in the preparation of the manuscript.

In addition, I want to acknowledge my debt to various assistants, chief among them Mr Gregory of Westminster Abbey, Mr Sharr ('Nelson') of St Paul's Cathedral and Mr Norton of Hampton Court Palace, without whose unfailing readiness to help, often in extremely difficult circumstances, many of the photographs could not have been taken.

Permission to reproduce a number of my photographs was kindly granted by *The Architectural Review* (Plates 30, 31, 33, 48), the *Society of Antiquaries* (Plates 42a and b), and the *Warburg Institute* (Plates 1–6, 8–10, 14, 15, 18–20b, 22–24b, 34–41, 43–47, 49, 50, 52–64. All the other photographs in the book are my own copyright.

CONTENTS

PART III

page

PHOTOGRAPHIC EQUIPMENT AND PRACTICAL CONSIDERATIONS

FOREWORD

I HAVE always been impressed by the title which, some sixty-five years ago, Lewis F. Day, one of the leading industrial designers of his time, gave to a collection of his essays. He called it *Everyday Art: Short Essays in the Arts Not-Fine*. Now photographs such as Mr Gernsheim's are unquestionably art, they are equally certainly every-day art, and they are, if I am not mistaken, what Lewis Day, not without pride, means by art not-fine.

Let us take these three assumptions one by one. As to the first, it may seem unnecessary to waste even one line of print on saying that photography is art. But the greatest thinkers on æsthetics during the years when photography appeared and, after all, brought forth almost at once such brilliant practitioners as Hill, Nadar and Mrs Cameron, were by no means convinced of any such claim. Ruskin, who had hailed photography as 'this most blessed invention' in a letter as early as 1845, was quick to add that 'a photograph is not a work of art, though it requires certain manipulations of paper and acid and subtle calculations of time' (*Stones of Venice,* Vol. III, 1853). For to Ruskin 'all art is great, and good, and fine, only so far as it is distinctively the work of *manhood* in its creative and highest sense' (ib.). He got a little muddled in this attitude because he was carried away by one of his chief grievances against his century, the grievance that it tended to 'substitute mechanism for skill' (*Lectures on Art*, Oxford, 1870), and photography to his mind was mechanism, painting skill. But his own definition of art as 'human labour regulated by human design' (ib.) confutes him. For how could the job of the photographer be better defined than by calling it labour regulated by design?

What blinded Ruskin to the possible æsthetic values of photography was of course his all-round dislike of anything dependent on machines. William Morris took this over and broadcast it so widely in his many lectures between 1877 and 1894 that much fighting by younger critics was needed to establish the artist who works for machine production, that is the designer as an artist in his own right. And as long as the designer is not appreciated *qua* designer, the photographer will not be appreciated *qua* photographer either.

For it is not enough to accept photography as an art. On the contrary, I would say that if the photographer thinks of himself as an artist and not as a designer, he will do a disservice to his own cause. The eminently skilful efforts of portrait and landscape photographers about 1900, as they were at that time praised by *The Studio*, were all directed towards competition with the modern painters of the day. But an impressionist picture depends entirely on the individual artist's handling of his brushes. The subtle haze, the dancing of touches and specks and commas as it enchants us in the canvases of painters like Whistler, or etchers like Pennell, must remain inaccessible to the artist who interposes a machine between his vision and his work.

And that is what the photographer does and has in common with those executants in the arts not-fine of whom Lewis Day speaks. The photograph is in the same relation to the painting as a piece of pottery to a piece of stone-carving. Comparisons are odious, and this, needless to say, is not better than most. It is indeed never fair to compare the peculiar interplay of mind, hand and machine in any one craft with that in another. But the fact remains that photography is, just as pottery is nowadays, one of the crafts which achieve their goal with the aid of machinery, and the great respect we have for the good photographer is connected with the respect for the designer as the man who is ready to put his æsthetic powers into the service of everyman, instead of playing them off in the seclusion of his private studio. A photograph is both art and commodity, as pots also are, but paintings are only rarely to-day. Where they are, say in the art of portraiture, there a comparison between the photographer's and the painter's approach, technique and limitations is especially rewarding, but it is outside the scope of this introduction to Mr Gernsheim's architectural and sculptural photographs.

And as far as the photography of buildings and statuary is concerned, there is obviously no question about its utilitarian function. Whenever Mr Gernsheim is asked to take a series of photographs of a church such as St Paul's or a house such as Ashburnham House or a monument such as that of Edward II at Gloucester, those who ask him want a record first and foremost, and he would be a bad photographer (though he may still get plenty of medals) if he went all out to produce spectacular prints in which relevant details are impressionistically blurred or post-impressionistically buried in the deep black which contrasts so well with strong high lights. The temptation must sometimes be great. The artist at the camera sees only too clearly what will make the most poignant picture, and a good deal of self-discipline and scientific conscience must be needed to give up the thrilling picture for the satisfactory picture.

In this of course the photographer is again in a position very similar to that of the designer. A novel chair may look wonderful with just that little of its outline developed into a billowing Henry Moorish curve, but if the chair thereby fails to be good to sit in, then the designer has not done a designer's (even if perhaps an abstract sculptor's) job.

Still – the dilemma is not really between functional and wonderful, or, to return to photography, between the thrilling and the satisfactory picture. What distinguishes Mr Gernsheim's photographs is, on the contrary, that they are both serving their recording purpose superlatively well and expressing the emotional qualities of the originals. He appears more an artist than merely a first-rate technician (or rather we tend to forget the technique because of the artistic quality) in such heads as that of Edward II (33), tragic, dissipated, Dostoiewskian; or that of Richard II (37), weak and sceptical; or that of Newton (53), sublimely visionary and yet strongly built; or finally that of Nelson (64), unforgettably vigorous, intrepid and defiant. All these characteristics must of course also exist in the originals, but who has ever seen them so intensely? If we don't, it may be for lack of æsthetic guidance, or for lack of access to so good a vantage point or simply for lack of good light. Here the photographer in recording becomes a mentor. His rôle changes into that of the conductor interpreting a score. Mr Gernsheim speaks in his book of the infinite patience necessary to get such shots. It is worth expending, if the results are so illuminating.

In this possibility of illuminating the meaning of a building or a work of sculpture lies the most fascinating problem for the photographer of architecture and statuary. He has to interpret works in themselves of æsthetic value, and interpret them in a different medium, two-dimensional instead of three-dimensional, and black and white instead of coloured, even if the colour of his original is only that of a veined marble or a number of many-shaded bricks or of flaking-off old stone as against restored, smooth new stone (30). To exemplify this duality of æsthetic qualities – qualities of the originals and qualities of the photographic prints, partly the same and partly quite different – let us take the photograph of the spiral stairs in St Paul's (4) which emphasizes all the elegance of the design and all the finesse of the workmanship and at the same time makes a delightful pattern in itself. Or take the view towards the south-west tower of St Paul's from the drum gallery (7). You may at first object and say that here the photographer has been taking liberties with the building to achieve that tremendous opposition of fat-lobed undulating leaves in the foreground and complicated angularity in the background. But that is not so. The

Wren who designed that tower towards the end of his life – he was over seventy then – would not have introduced these diagonally jutting-out columns and these convex bays in between, and again the discord between this convexness and the concaveness of the little intermediate stage above, if he had not enjoyed baroque drama and the interplay of curves and angles. Similarly I would not call it a liberty to let appear behind the fantastic catacombs of Highgate Cemetery with their pyramidal corner tower the spire of Vulliamy's neo-Gothic church (9). For variety and mixture were evidently just the things which the designer of this piece of macabre, operatic gloom – was it Geary, was it Bunning? – delighted in.

Reference to these few examples has, I hope, made it clear how, in the ideal case, recording accuracy is blended with sensitive interpretation of the meaning of a three-dimensional work of art and with the creation of an independent work of two-dimensional design. Of these three aspects under which a photograph of sculpture or architecture should be criticized, it will as a rule be comparatively easy to reach agreement on the first and the third. Does the photograph show precisely what is there? And does it make a good, an æsthetically good, pattern in form and tone? These questions will be answered much more confidently than the other: Is the photographer's a legitimate presentation of the architect's or sculptor's intentions? The case of Plates 60a and 60b and Mr Gernsheim's comment on them shows that occasionally the historically more competent and the visually more competent expert cannot convince each other at all.*

The power of the photographer to strengthen or destroy the original is at any rate undeniable. In a building the choice of the views, then of the angles, then of the light, simply makes the building. It can let the nave of a church appear tall and narrow or broad and squat – almost regardless of its real proportions. And, what is more, it can bring out a detail so forcefully that it carries more conviction on the plate than in the original. The possibility of 'isolating details from surroundings', as Mr Gernsheim puts it, is in my opinion the photographer's greatest privilege. He can stop you to concentrate on something which the eye roving over the whole of a wall or a statue may miss completely. Look, he says, here are some early bits of Renaissance detail in a vault still in all its essentials Gothic in character (15), and here is the noble restraint of a pediment designed a hundred years later perhaps by Inigo Jones himself (23), and here the inexhaustible richness of floral

* I am with Dr Wittkower and not Mr Gernsheim. If Scheemakers has failed to make Shakespeare's face look the face of a genius, the photograph should in my opinion not bring in the genius which the sculptor of the statue has been lacking in.

detail in a Grinling Gibbons carving (48), and there the crispness of late 18th century neo-Greek at its best (19b). Study the detail of the exquisite ornamentation in the gallery as the photograph allows you to or perhaps compels you to, and as inside Greenwich Chapel only one in a thousand would have the inquisitiveness and the patience to do, and the spirit of the whole work, its period style and its personal style, will *in nuce* be revealed to you.

Nikolaus Pevsner

PART I

THE PHOTOGRAPHY OF ARCHITECTURE AND SCULPTURE IN GREAT BRITAIN FROM FOX TALBOT TO THE PRESENT DAY

THE photography of architecture is as old as the art of photography itself, for Fox Talbot, the originator of the photographic process as practised to-day, was the first in this field. In his account of the 'Art of Photogenic Drawing' which he read to the Royal Society on 31st January 1839, he mentioned that Lacock Abbey, his residence in Wiltshire, was the first building that was ever known to have drawn its own picture. Only one of these tiny representations survives. It is the earliest extant photograph in the world, taken in the summer of 1835.

APPRECIATION OF 'SUN-PICTURES'

Before 1839, works of art and architecture were recorded exclusively by means of engravings, lithographs, aquatints and mezzotints. Photography first made possible the wide distribution of faithful representations, and the public was eager to possess 'photographic drawings' or 'sun-pictures' of buildings which they so far knew only from travellers' descriptions or fictitious engravings. 'Even accomplished artists', wrote Fox Talbot in 1844, 'now avail themselves of an invention which delineates in a few moments the almost endless details of Gothic architecture which a whole day would hardly suffice to draw correctly in the ordinary manner.'

Talbot's scientific friend Sir David Brewster gave his opinion that 'The home-faring man, whom fate or duty chains to his birthplace, will, without the fatigues and dangers of travel, scan the beauties and wonders of the globe, not in the fantastic or deceitful images of a hurried pencil, but in the very picture which would have been printed on his own retina, were he magically transported to the scene.' He points out the scenes of interest which he had in mind – 'The palaces of sovereigns, the edifices of social life, the temples of religion, the watchtowers of war, the obelisks of fame, and the mausolea of domestic grief', all of which 'remained under the blue cupola of nature's museum' and therefore formed subjects which were not only *worthy* of being photographed but, what was more important, *could* be photographed. For it was chiefly the lack of sensitivity of the daguerreotype and calotype processes – and in England also stringent patent restrictions – which compelled the choice of inanimate subjects.

PHOTOGRAPHY FOR BOOK ILLUSTRATION

In France, the first book with illustrations based on the new art – *Paris et ses Environs réproduits par le Daguerréotype* – appeared in 1840. Owing to the impossibility of reproducing daguerreotypes, it consisted of lithographic prints copied from them. It was Fox Talbot who first used actual photographs for book illustration in his *Pencil of Nature*, which was issued in parts beginning in July 1844. At about the same time he put photographic views on the market in competition with engravings. For this purpose he had built at Reading towards the end of 1843 or early in 1844 one of the first photographic 'glass-houses', an establishment where photography was undertaken commercially and copies printed from his and other people's negatives. In collaboration with the Rev. Calvert Jones and Nicholas Henneman (Talbot's former valet, now turned photographer) and with the help of a number of other 'converts', Talbot took a large number of photographs of sculpture and public buildings in London, Oxford, Cambridge, York, Chester, Dublin, Paris, etc, copies of which were advertised for sale 'at most respectable print-sellers or stationers in the Kingdom'. The advertisement is interesting from another point of view, for it states that 'the prices affixed are very moderate, in order that all who are interested in the progress of art may possess themselves of specimens'.

In Part I of *The Pencil of Nature,* Talbot included two architectural subjects – views of Queen's College, Oxford, and the Boulevard des Italiens, Paris. He also showed one of the earliest photographs of sculpture – a bust of Patroclus, about which Talbot made some very interesting technical observations which are essentially as correct to-day as when they were written.

> 'Statues, busts and other specimens of sculpture are generally well represented by the photographic art; and also very rapidly, in consequence of their whiteness.
>
> These delineations are susceptible of an almost unlimited variety; since in the first place a statue may be placed in any position with regard to the sun, either directly opposite to it or at an angle – the directness or obliquity of the illumination causing of course an immense difference in the effect. And when a choice has been made of the direction in which the sun's rays shall fall, the statue may be then turned round on its pedestal, which produces a second set of variations no less considerable

than the first. And when to this is added the change of size which is produced in the image by bringing the camera obscura nearer to the statue, or removing it further off, it becomes evident how very great a number of different effects may be obtained from a single specimen of sculpture.

With regard to many statues, however, a better effect is obtained by delineating them in cloudy weather than in sunshine– for the sunshine causes such strong shadows as sometimes to confuse the subject. To prevent this it is a good plan to hold a white cloth on one side of the statue at a little distance, to reflect back the sun's rays and cast a faint illumination on the parts which would otherwise be lost in shadow.'

TWO KINDS OF PHOTOGRAPHY

To-day the photography of architecture and sculpture is mainly practised by professionals who have made it a specialised study, but in the early days of photography it was the main field–apart from landscapes–to which photographers in general devoted their time. Although the majority were satisfied with the mere recording of facts, a few tried to interpret their subjects and produced photographs of great pictorial value which can still fire our imagination to-day. So there was, right from the beginning, a clear division between mechanical and artistic photographers, and a subject appears insipid or interesting in their photographs according to the amount of thought and artistic feeling which went into the making of the picture.

EARLY ARCHITECTURAL PHOTOGRAPHERS

David Octavius Hill is chiefly known for the beautiful portraits which he took in collaboration with Robert Adamson between 1843 and 1848, but his work also includes a considerable number of architectural views of Edinburgh and St Andrews. In fact, it must be assumed that Hill started photography as early as 1841, for he took views of the progress of the building of the Scott Monument, on which work had begun in the summer of that year.

The Rev. Calvert Jones, a friend and close collaborator of Talbot, took architectural views of Rome and Malta between 1843 and 1845.

A. Claudet, N. Henneman, Philip Delamotte and J. E. Mayall produced excellent exterior and interior views of the Crystal Palace at the time of the 1851 Exhibition—Claudet taking stereoscopic daguerreotypes, Henneman employing the Talbotype, Delamotte the waxed paper and Mayall the albumen-on-glass process.

The following year Roger Fenton was commissioned to go to Russia to take photographs of the suspension bridge which was being built by an English engineer across the Dnieper at Kieff. He took the opportunity to visit St Petersburg and Moscow and brought home many splendid photographs of Russian church architecture and the Kremlin. Fenton was certainly one of the most versatile artists, for hardly had he returned from photographing the Crimean War when he started (in 1856) his work for the Trustees of the British Museum, photographing the Elgin Marbles and Roman sculpture, as well as other art treasures. Between 1856 and his retirement from photography in 1862, Fenton took a fine series of photographs of English cathedrals, abbeys, and famous country houses.

In the early fifties Dr Thomas Keith, an Edinburgh surgeon, produced beautiful calotype views of the Scottish capital and its surroundings. Though his work has hitherto remained entirely unknown, a collection of his magnificent 10″ × 12″ waxed paper negatives which came by chance into my hands shows him to be one of the greatest masters of architectural photography who ever lived. Artistically and technically his photographs are equal to those of D. O. Hill and Robert Adamson. They have the same poetic charm, breadth and artistic vision which are universally admired in Hill's portraits.

About the same time James Robertson, who was chief engraver to the Imperial Mint in Constantinople, published views of that city, of Malta and of Athens. They do not, however, rise to greater heights than accurate records.

Charles Clifford, living in Madrid, aroused great admiration in the mid-fifties with his views of Spanish architecture. R. MacPherson and later James Anderson, two Scots, became the leading photographers in Rome. Though that city probably contains more picturesque material than any other in the world, MacPherson and Anderson disdained to descend to mere prettiness in their treatment of it. Careful observation of the play of light and shade lends life to the mouldering grandeur of these Roman subjects. MacPherson ranks in my opinion as the greatest architectural photographer of the early period.

Francis Frith deserves high praise for his photographs of ancient temples and monumental sculpture in Egypt and Palestine in 1857/58, and Ethiopia in 1860. He was one of the most energetic photographers of the period. In the early 'sixties he travelled with his camera over half Europe, issuing his views as his own publisher in books, portfolios and albums. With some exceptions, however, his work was largely recording– nor could so prolific a photographer have done much more.

Samuel Bourne (Simla), Dr J. Murray (Agra), James Fergusson (Calcutta) and Capt. L. Tripe, the Government photographer in Madura, all chronicled the manifold phases of Hindu and Mohammedan architecture in India, displaying great artistic skill and a thorough understanding of architectural principles.

Lastly, mention must be made of Francis Bedford and G. W. Wilson, who each took a series of exterior and interior photographs of English cathedrals over a number of years, starting in the late eighteen-fifties.

Space does not allow me to enumerate more than the most outstanding architectural photographers in the first twenty-five years of photography.

DECLINE OF ARCHITECTURAL PHOTOGRAPHY

During the next twenty-five years not a single new architectural photographer worth mentioning appears on the scene. The first excitement of the new art had evaporated; photography had become a flourishing trade.

Two events had occurred some years previously, which began slowly but ever increasingly to have a deteriorating effect on architectural photography.

The first event was Talbot's defeat in 1854 in his claim to the collodion process, invented by Frederick Scott Archer and given free to the world in 1851. In England photography had been shackled by Daguerre's and Talbot's patents of 1839 and 1841 respectively, and portrait photography was a 'closed shop' until 1854 for all except a few men of means and ability who opened studios in the principal towns, for which they paid very high licence fees to the patentees. With the restrictions now gone, there was an onrush of people who wished to make their living by photography. They realised, however, that much more money was to be made out of man's vanity than out of mankind's cultural heritage, and soon portrait studios sprang up everywhere like mushrooms after rain.

The second factor was the tremendous popularity of the stereoscope in the late 'fifties. This led to a steady decline in the production and sale of large photographic prints, which were now superseded by the small stereoscopic slides. The craze for the stereoscope was infectious; like the family album, it found its way into every Victorian household. It brought in its train a completely different approach to photography. Previously the large prints had been admired for their beauty, whereas the most important quality required of the small stereoscopic pictures was a realistic effect when viewed through the instrument. Naturally less time and trouble went into the making of these stereoscopic slides, which were manufactured and sold by the thousand. Quality gave way to quantity, as in all cases where mass production replaces individual craftsmanship.

In addition, greatly improved photographic methods attracted quite a different class of persons to take up the art. The rapidity of production, of which the merely mechanical process of photographic picture making is capable, became a source of great mischief. Many of the enthusiastic 'amateur gentlemen' of the first period – the clergymen, doctors, lawyers and artists – had retired, and the 'new class of persons', sighed Francis Frith in 1859, 'now a very large one, who practise photography, is undoubtedly a very different class from the old régime.' A natural consequence of the greater commercialisation of photography was that it fell into the hands of tradesmen who were out to make easy money, and who neither desired, nor were mentally equipped, to produce pictures.

BOOKS ON ARCHITECTURAL SUBJECTS

In the early 'sixties numerous books on architectural subjects made their appearance, and for the price formerly paid for four to six large mounted prints, an expertly written and photographically illustrated book could now be bought. Space allows me to mention only one of the most popular: *Ruined Abbeys and Castles of Great Britain and Ireland*, by William and Mary Howitt, which was published in two volumes, each illustrated with twenty-six original photographs glued in between the text of the book. Though some famous photographers of the day – Bedford, Fenton, Ogle, Sedgfield and Wilson – contributed to this book, the cold hand of commercialism is evident in every picture. The moment photographs shrank to the size and status of mere illustrations, their pictorial quality deteriorated.

THE FORERUNNERS OF PICTURE POSTCARDS

Almost simultaneously with the extended application of photography to book illustration we find the establishment of a few large firms of art photographers like Joseph Cundall in London, Francis Frith in Reigate, and James Valentine in Dundee, who employed a staff of photographers travelling round the country, and soon had for sale cheap photographic views of the most famous buildings in Britain – the forerunners of the present-day picture postcards.

In addition to this necessarily sketchy résumé of individual activity in architectural photography, the part played by a number of societies which were working for a wider dissemination of art knowledge must be briefly outlined.

THE ANTIQUARIAN PHOTOGRAPHIC CLUB

In 1854 the Antiquarian Photographic Club was formed for the purpose of making periodical excursions into the country to secure accurate views of objects of antiquarian interest. This was no doubt the most exclusive photographic club that ever existed – only Fellows of the Royal Society or of the Society of Antiquaries, and Members of the Royal Institution, were eligible for membership, and furthermore had to be elected unanimously. All three Institutions were chiefly concerned with research, and a copy of every photograph taken was deposited in the portfolios of the Society of Antiquaries. Whatever the value of the results to archæology may have been at the time, we would not be surprised to learn that the photographs were exceedingly dull.*

A noteworthy contribution to the photography of architecture was made in 1855 by the Rev. F. A. S. Marshall with his pamphlet *Photography: the importance of its application in preserving pictorial records of the National Monuments of History and Art*, which is, as far as I know, the first publication to draw attention to the importance of this specialised subject, and to which was appended *A practical description of the Talbotype process as adopted and practised by the author during the last seven years.*

THE ARCHITECTURAL PHOTOGRAPHIC ASSOCIATION

Two years later the Architectural Photographic Association was inaugurated in London. In their report it was stated that 'The peculiar value of photography as a means of obtaining representations of architectural subjects has for some time attracted much attention, and now that this marvellous art has both attained to so high a degree of perfection and its treatment is also so generally understood, the present period appears to be most favourable for the foundation of this Association.' Affiliated groups were formed in the same year in Scotland and Ireland, as well as in a great many English provincial cities and towns. On the committee charged with the duty of forming the Association we find such famous architects as Sir Charles Barry and Mr (later Sir) George Gilbert Scott. The Association was under the presidency of Professor Cockerell, and had as its main purpose the formation of a national collection of architectural photographs of famous buildings in Britain and abroad. To this end the co-operation was obtained of the photographic departments of the Board of Ordnance (Royal Engineers) and of the East India Company, as well as of a number of eminent photographers at home and abroad (e.g. the brothers Alinari in Florence).

When the first exhibition of the Architectural Photographic Association was opened in January 1858 it was prophesied that 'This grand collection of architectural

* A search was made for them, at my request, by the librarian of the Society of Antiquaries, but without success

photographs must speedily exercise a powerful influence upon the art education of all persons who either practise architecture as a profession or take an interest in it as a great and noble art. A few years may be expected to produce a really magnificent assemblage of these most beautiful and most interesting and instructive pictures, thus forming throughout the Empire National Galleries of architectural art.' The only criticisms the *Art Journal* ventured to make were the lack of interior views and the want of details, for it was felt that 'in order to promote the best interests of architecture, each more important general feature of any great building, or of any part of a great building, should be attended by a series of views of details given on a scale sufficiently large to exhibit *their* details with all that wonderful minuteness and precision which are the characteristics of photography.'

The lack of detail photographs is, however, not apparent in architectural photography alone; it is equally manifest in all other branches of photography of the early period, and was partly due to technical difficulties and partly to the fact that there was no popular demand. The modern close-up, as envisaged by the *Art Journal*, has come into fashion in still-photography only comparatively recently, and is due to the influence of the cinematograph.

The absence of interior views was explained by the *Photographic News* in February 1859: 'Interior architectural subjects are a department of photography which we need hardly inform our readers is one of the most difficult to obtain any great amount of success in. Sometimes one obtains results which would please the most fastidious, while at other times the pictures are by no means as satisfactory as we should desire: this we apprehend is not so much from a fault of manipulation as from the photographer attempting a subject which would be almost certain to meet with failure.' The great unevenness of light distribution in a room and the enormous light contrasts near windows were an insuperable difficulty at a time when plates were not yet backed against halation. Also there was no practical form of artificial light in those days which a photographer could have used, with the result that exposures lasted several hours. MacPherson tells us that in one or two cases an exposure of *two days* was necessary to produce a good negative.* Even magnesium light, which was put on the market in 1864, did not become a practical proposition for the photography of interiors, as it generated a great deal of smoke and was exceedingly difficult to handle. To my knowledge, it was used only twice for this purpose, namely by the Astronomer Royal for Scotland, Piazzi Smyth, in 1865, when photographing

* *Photographic Journal*, 15th December 1862, p.184

the interior of the Great Pyramid, and by the Jackson brothers, who experimented with it in Bradford Colliery in May of the same year.*

THE ARUNDEL SOCIETY

In addition to the Antiquarian Photographic Club and the Architectural Photographic Association, the Arundel Society made a great effort for the popular diffusion of works of art at a cheap price. For this purpose they instituted a photographic department and appointed Messrs Cundall of the Photographic Institution as their photographers, whose task it was to photograph selected objects in various museums, public buildings, cathedrals and private collections at home and abroad.

The Arundel Society also acted as publishing agents for the Department of Science and Art of the South Kensington Museum (now the Victoria and Albert Museum), which was the first public museum in Britain to open a photographic department (in October 1859). The primary object of the department was to furnish the eighty Government art schools with cheap reproductions of items in the collections of the British Museum and the South Kensington Museum; but after providing for the art schools it was thought right to give the public at large the benefit of the photographs at cost price, for the promotion of general art education. The public certainly took advantage of this offer, for it is stated that the total number of copies sold between October 1859 and October 1862 was 24,500. Anyone wishing to have an object in these museums specially photographed could order negatives, which became his property, at the rate of only 3d per square inch. The Museum's photographer was Thurston Thompson. Roger Fenton's photographs of art treasures in the British Museum were also sold at South Kensington. By 1869 the Department possessed a library of 24,000 photographs of the most remarkable existing works of architecture, painting, sculpture and decorative art.

THE ARCHITECTURAL PHOTOGRAPHIC SOCIETY

In 1868 the reconstituted Architectural Photographic Society (as the Association was now called) went a step further in their efforts to procure the best possible

*I refer here, of course, to the early period. It was only after 1890 when Robert Slingsby published his *Treatise on Magnesium Flash-light Photography* that its application was considered practicable to any extent. H. Bedford Lemere mentioned, for instance, at a meeting at the Royal Photographic Society in 1897 that he found flashlight of considerable assistance when photographing large interiors, particularly during the dull season of the year, and he cited an instance when he lighted an apartment – after an exposure of 3½ hours – for two to three minutes by means of magnesium ribbon for the purpose of picking up detail and getting a little highlight photographs. It was felt that notwithstanding the *technical* excellence of the photographs, the points of view were not always chosen by its members with sound judgment and good taste, and that they needed the guidance of an experienced architect if they were to achieve a collection of photographs of subjects which a professional architect would desire to record. It was realised also that without proper planning there was too much duplication of favourite buildings. It was therefore decided to concentrate on the systematic recording of one particular district at a time.

A PHOTOGRAPHIC TOUR OF THE RHINELAND

For the first photographic tour the Rhineland was selected in order to procure a series of photographs of Romanesque and early Transition work. The Society's report reads rather like a military operation, and I cannot refrain from quoting it. 'Koblenz was fixed as the headquarters of this very interesting expedition, round which the photographic excursions were to revolve. Most of the places on the banks of the Rhine from Cologne to Bingen were visited and explored by Mr Seddon (the accomplished architect) before the arrival of the photographers on the scene of their future operations. So also were the banks of the Lahn as far as Limburg and those of the Moselle as far as Münster-Maifeld, and thus when the whole working force had assembled it was a comparatively easy matter to form the actual plan of action.'

If we were to inquire into the quality of the photographs achieved we would have to admit that the great majority which have survived do not go beyond good honest record work. The artistic capacity of the man behind the camera, on which the effectiveness of a photograph almost entirely depends, was either non-existent or could not find a way of expression, for such conducted tours as that described were certainly not conducive to originality and individuality.

Mention should also be made of the Society for Photographing the Relics of Old London, which did valuable work in the 1870's and '80's, in recording much of Old London, which was then so rapidly disappearing. Their photographs, which were issued in sets to which the South Kensington Museum (now the Victoria and Albert Museum), the Guildhall Library, and the library of the Royal Academy were subscribers, among others, have gained considerably in historical value. Since they were issued, the face of London has again changed greatly, and as the years go by, more and more charming old bits will disappear, to be replaced by stereotyped chain-stores or modern office blocks.

THE WORK OF F. H. EVANS

In the last quarter of the century amateur photographers spent all their efforts in producing 'salon' pictures of the artificial and sentimental kind then so much in favour, in direct competition with their brethren at the Royal Academy. The photography of architecture and sculpture now had little appeal; it was cold-shouldered as 'record work' or treated 'pictorially', i.e. architectural themes served merely for studies in light and atmosphere. It was not long before they were debased into cheap effect pictures of the kind which still occasionally does the round of exhibitions: a tomb lit up by a shaft of sunlight which has been 'pictorially improved' by shaking out an old sack or some such dusty article just before the exposure. This in fact was the advice offered by a photographer to his 'artist' friends, and judging from the mass production of such architectural pictures the tip was eagerly followed. When, therefore, towards the end of the century Frederick H. Evans exhibited his first pictures of cathedrals, he caused no little stir, for the magnificent quality of his platinotypes and the excellence of his vision had at once to be admitted, and in succeeding years a new appreciation of architectural photography arose, no doubt stimulated by his work.

Evans, who laboured at the time of pictorial photography's fight for recognition as a means of personal expression relying mainly on handwork, believed, curiously enough, in straight and pure technique. His finest work is exemplified in his photographs of the most important cathedrals in England and France, and though an amateur, he remained the foremost figure in the architectural field for the next twenty-five years.

ERNEST MARRIAGE

Mention must also be made of Ernest Marriage, chiefly for his book *The Sculptures of Chartres Cathedral* published in 1909. This book contains 120 illustrations taken from 1901 on, and they are worth studying even to-day, though we now have that magnificent portfolio of photographs of the same cathedral published by Editions Tel (1938). Marriage's work consists chiefly of detail photographs on a scale not previously attempted – though not yet details of details. He was a great propagandist for the telephoto lens, on which he wrote a treatise, and he astonished a meeting of photographers in 1897 with his statement that 'porches and doorways of cathedrals will often contain more interesting details than the rest of the buildings afford.' Just before the First World War he took a large series of photographs of the carvings of Amiens Cathedral.

R. H. WEAVER

Inspired by Evans's work, Mr R. H. Weaver (now President of Trinity College, Oxford) took at various times between 1913 and 1931 a most impressive series of photographs of cathedrals and other ecclesiastical buildings of medieval Spain. His superb platinotypes, which we had an opportunity of seeing a few years ago at the Royal Photographic Society, showed that Mr Weaver's powers of interpretation and technical accomplishment are in every respect equal to those of his friend and master.

Compared with Evans and Weaver, H. Bedford Lemere's work is more prosaic. He commenced his photographs of London's historic churches and other buildings about 1890, and remained for the next forty or fifty years the leading commercial architectural photographer in this country.

THE NATIONAL PHOTOGRAPHIC RECORD ASSOCIATION

Ever since W. Jerome Harrison's *Proposal for a National Photographic Record and Survey** in 1892, there was much talk about establishing such an organisation. But it was not until 1895 that a committee was formed and Leon Vidal, head of the Musée des Photographies Documentaires, was invited to attend a conference in London and to report on the work of the French organisation.

An important step towards its formation was the acceptance two years later by the British Museum authorities from Sir J. Benjamin Stone of 100 platinotype views of Westminster Abbey, which were deposited in the Print Department. Soon afterwards the National Photographic Record Association was formed, due to the untiring efforts of Sir Benjamin Stone, who combined with equal enthusiasm the position of president and chief photographer, besides being a Member of Parliament. The Association's aims were not confined to recording architecture and objects of historic interest but included photographic documentation of folk customs etc. In order to ensure that the record would be of value to posterity, it was stipulated that all photographs should be done in one of the permanent printing processes such as carbon or platinotype. The Association deposited the results of their labours in the Print Department of the British Museum – a circumstance due, no doubt, to the fact that the Museum's director was also a member of the council of the Association. In 1909 a figure of 4000 photographs was mentioned, but after a further short life the work of the Association petered out, chiefly on account of the apathy of its members, about which its keen president more than once bitterly complained.

* *Photographic Journal*, 28th May 1892, p.226-242

THE NATIONAL BUILDINGS RECORD

It was not until the Second World War that the urgency of external circumstances gave rise to the formation of a new scheme which found national support. When at the time of the destruction of a great many Wren churches and other priceless buildings during the blitz, it had become evident that in the absence of proper records the contribution to our culture and history of much of our national heritage would be largely effaced, the National Buildings Record – a central organisation for the recording of English architecture and monuments – was at long last formed (February 1941). One of its tasks was to co-ordinate existing photographic records, for in an emergency so great it was obvious that all organisations which had in the past commissioned architectural photographs should put their resources at the disposal of the National collection. The response to a much-publicised appeal was great – many County Committees were formed, and professional and amateur photographers alike devoted much of their spare time to the recording of local buildings and monuments. In addition, various funds made it possible for the National Buildings Record to employ a small staff of photographers, and to commission others in various parts of the country in specific programmes of work.

Thus the ambitious scheme initiated by the Architectural Photographic Association in 1857, which foundered after some years through lack of funds, was successfully revived on a larger scale; and although England was far behind its Continental neighbours in setting up a central organisation for a comprehensive survey of its art treasures, the National Buildings Record rapidly grew into an important institution from what was a modest beginning in 1941.

By June 1944, when a comprehensive exhibition was arranged at the National Gallery, the collection was said to have reached the large total of 215,000 items, and it has since been considerably enlarged. In January 1949 the total number of photographs in their possession was stated to be 315,500.

To complete this survey we have to mention the valuable contributions in the architectural field which continue to be made, as in the past, by *The Architectural Review* and *Country Life*. Reference must also be made to the work done by the Central Council for the Care of Churches, the Georgian Group, the London Survey, the Wren Society, and the Royal Commission on Historical Monuments; and among photographers, foremost to Messrs Dell & Wainwright, Mr Herbert Felton and Miss Margaret Harker.

THE WARBURG INSTITUTE

Among other organisations, the Warburg Institute (London University) was asked to collaborate in the N.B.R. scheme, and in February 1942 I joined their staff for this purpose. Advised on art matters by an art historian, Dr R. Wittkower, I undertook in the next three-and-a-half years complete photographic surveys of many of the most important buildings and monuments in the London area. The series started with the monuments in Westminster Abbey and was followed by a comprehensive survey of the architecture and monuments of St Paul's Cathedral; the architecture of the British Museum; the Royal effigies from Henry VII's Chapel; the Royal Naval College, Greenwich; Hampton Court Palace; St Martin's-in-the-Fields and a number of other churches; 10 Downing Street; the Treasury; Chiswick House and Park; and several famous clubs and other places of architectural or historic interest.

Each survey took anything from a few weeks to several months. The longest was Hampton Court Palace with six months, whilst I took the largest number of negatives (about four hundred) during three-and-a-half months' work at Westminster Abbey. In all, I took approximately sixteen hundred photographs for the Warburg Institute.

In the choice of illustrations for this book I was guided not so much by importance of subject matter as by their photographic appeal and instructional value for those intending to specialise in architectural and sculptural photography. Though the sculpture section could have been filled with African, Chinese, Indian or modern sculpture alone, it was decided to restrict it chiefly to English monumental sculpture because of its wider appeal.

PART II

AN INTRODUCTION TO THE PHOTOGRAPHY OF ARCHITECTURE AND SCULPTURE

ARCHITECTURE and sculpture are too often admired only for the historical associations they arouse, for their fame, for their antiquarian value, or for their intricacy of workmanship. Few people enjoy architecture and sculpture purely as works of art. This is partly due to our educational system, which is too little concerned with visual values, and partly to the poor illustrations in many of the books written by antiquarian-minded art historians. These photographs are usually taken by a commercial photographer with an eye untrained for, or completely insensitive to, the beauty and spirit of a work of art, or sometimes by the art historian himself, unversed in the technicalities of photography, and only interested in having a straightforward record which will just suffice as illustration to his writing.

TOWARDS A HIGHER QUALITY IN PHOTOGRAPHY

This book was prompted by a desire to stimulate a higher quality in architectural and sculptural photography than that to which we are accustomed. There is obviously little sense in amassing hundreds of thousands of photographs in one big national record, if the great majority of them continue, as hitherto, to be commercial hack-work and amateur snapshots, lacking æsthetic appeal and failing to stimulate an awareness and appreciation of the great treasures which this country possesses, and which have so far remained largely unknown to the general public.

It is my firm belief that a photographer who is unable to appreciate the beauty of a work of art will not be able to re-create it for the appreciation of others. Only when he has acquired a certain knowledge of art and understanding of the artist's intentions can he convey its meaning. Whether his representation is 'dead' or 'alive' depends on his viewpoint, on his lighting, on his feeling for the material. Our appreciation is, in fact, conditioned by the photographer's interpretation, much in the same way as intelligent enjoyment of music is dependent upon the interpretive powers of soloist or conductor. Through a new experience, an original outlook, the eye as well as the mind can discover fresh meaning, and just as the significance of a musical phrase may suddenly be understood for the first time during an inspired performance, so the significance of the beauty of a familiar architectural detail, which may have almost disappeared through its subordination to the larger design, may suddenly reveal itself in a close-up. Such experiences cannot fail to enrich the imagination, and through it stimulate a more sympathetic and appreciative understanding of the creative mind. Art appreciation will, it is hoped, rapidly grow with a visual re-education which is based on inspired photographs.

THE VALUE OF VISUAL EDUCATION

In the following pages it is not intended to trouble the reader with *general* considerations of what to photograph and how to do it. The plates and the notes accompanying them will, it is hoped, elucidate theoretical considerations. My remarks are confined to methods and some practical hints I have gained by experience, hoping that the more thorny problems of composition and approach will become self-evident through the illustrations. I cannot too strongly recommend the intending photographer to study thoroughly the work of the architects and artists who built or embellished our cathedrals and our country houses and designed or sculptured our historic monuments. At the same time, it is of the utmost importance that he should study the photographs of such acknowledged masters in this field as Evans, Weaver and Bedford Lemere, to whom I would like to add the names of a few outstanding photographers outside Britain – Sougez and André Vigneau in France; Professor Walter Hege and Kurt Hielscher in Germany; Dr Martin Hürlimann in Switzerland; G. F. Kidder-Smith in the U.S.A.; and the Czech photographer Karel Klicka, who has recently given us that magnificent picture book of Prague, *City of Baroque and Gothic*. From them the aspiring photographer will learn infinitely more than from the perusal of innumerable textbooks. I attach little value to dogmatic teaching; there are exceptions to every rule, and the exceptions sometimes prove more important than the rule itself. As the photographer gains experience, his knowledge widens and he discovers again and again that many of the instructions he has read have only a relative value, and that he has to approach each subject afresh and individually and always under varying conditions.

PHOTOGRAPHY OF ARCHITECTURE AND SCULPTURE

GENERAL CONSIDERATIONS

What value can be attached to such general textbook statements as the following? 'The camera should not be set up in the centre of an aisle or colonnade, but a little to one side or another'; or, 'an unusual standpoint should be avoided' for 'The architect built his work to be seen from the height of the eye, and if we are to avoid an unnatural appearance in the print, the camera should view it from a similar position.' Had I ever taken such futile instructions to heart, ninety-nine out of a hundred of my photographs would not have been taken. On the other hand, originality for its own sake is equally mistaken. Some years ago I saw a series of interior views of a cathedral which were taken from under the central tower in all four directions. These photographs naturally completely failed to convey a correct impression of the cathedral's interior, for they gave in each case only a truncated view instead of the whole. The same applies, of course, to detail photographs: important architectural features must not be shown in a truncated form; a heavy arch should not appear as though floating in the air, but part of its supporting pier or column should be included. The photographer should avoid any feeling of want of support or instability, and this applies particularly to the much-abused tilting of the camera, resulting in photographs which give the beholder the uncomfortable notion that it might be unsafe to enter the building.

THE PHOTOGRAPHER MUST UNDERSTAND HIS SUBJECT

The photographer who makes architecture his field of activity has to know something of the history of the building which he intends to record, and understand the period of architecture to which it belongs. And though a good working knowledge of styles and constructional forms is essential to a clear understanding and right approach, artistic susceptibility is even more important. He has to comprehend something of what was in the mind and soul of the architect who planned the structure. Consideration has to be given to form, perspective, proportion and spacing of architecture. The importance of understanding its function, its character, its general mass, its ornament – or lack of ornament – cannot be too strongly emphasised. It is only through such knowledge that the photographer can intelligently relate the general plan of a building to its parts and give a correct interpretation. In contemporary work co-operation with the architect or sculptor is, wherever possible, of the greatest value, in order to achieve an authentic interpretation. It should not be assumed that a photographer – or a critic! – can grasp in five or ten minutes what took the sculptor or architect months or years to create.

FINDING THE BEST VIEWPOINT

A building or a piece of sculpture will often be designed to look its best from a certain viewpoint. It is that point which the photographer must try to find, through careful study and under various lighting conditions, before making his exposure. The knack of getting the best view from the right standpoint and in the correct lighting, or in other words, of knowing the most favourable conditions, and reproducing them in the photograph, is a process of trained observation.

SELECTION AND SIMPLIFICATION

A good photograph can only be achieved by a process of selection and simplification. Whatever is included in it must have significance. For the organic whole there may well be one viewpoint only which is the best, but the unusual can only be explored by not sticking to a fixed viewpoint all the time. Walking round the building or the piece of sculpture, one will often discover unexpected pleasures. To photograph a building from a slight angle will usually convey a better impression of its proportions and volume than a direct frontal view. A seventeenth or eighteenth century building, on the other hand, is probably designed for being seen centrally. It usually has a symmetrical layout, and it might be wrong to spoil this intentional symmetry by introducing an asymmetrical viewpoint.

THE WEATHER

It will be evident from the nature of the work that the weather plays a most important rôle in the architectural photographer's life. Generally speaking, outdoor photographs should not be taken on a dull day: only sunlight lends life to form. The photographer may have to wait for days or even weeks until conditions are as he wants them, but it will repay the trouble. Sometimes I have spent days at an hotel hoping that the sun would break through, and more than once it happened that I returned to London after several days of fruitless waiting, only to find that the very next day was fine and sunny.

CHOOSING THE RIGHT TIME OF DAY

During almost every hour of the day the appearance of a building varies with the play of sunlight upon its principal or lateral façades, and careful planning is half the success of a photograph. Nothing must be left to chance. The factor of luck should not enter into the photographer's work at all – though he may call it luck that the ladder from which he worked did not collapse, or that the electric light did not fuse just during the exposure, as it is wont to do.

The pictorial photographer will choose the hour for taking his view when the building has the best light. The record photographer will take his view at any hour indifferently, but the resulting picture will clearly proclaim by which of the two it was taken.

The best way of deciding upon the most suitable time for photographing is to pay a preliminary visit to the building in question and study the light conditions on the spot. A façade facing east has its best light in the mid-morning, a building facing north, late in the afternoon or early evening, and even then it may get sunlight only during the summer months. A careful study of the continually changing effect of sunlight upon the building will often show that the exposure can only be made at a certain season of the year.

The picture must be taken in such a way as clearly to show the structure of the building. Side light is always the best: having the sun at one's back results in a flat and insipid picture, lacking relief and brilliance. However, in exceptional cases a strong relief effect may also be obtained indirectly, i.e. not on the building itself through the play of sunlight, but by throwing the main façade into relief through the contrast of adjoining buildings in shadow. (See Plate 31).

PLANNING

When it is impossible to make a personal inspection beforehand, it will pay to study a street plan and ascertain the position of the building and its aspect.

How essential it is to plan in advance can perhaps be best illustrated by a personal experience. In 1938 I was commissioned by a leading shipping company to go on a Mediterranean cruise, visiting Athens, Istanbul, Dubrovnik and Venice, in order to take some new publicity photographs. Bearing in mind that I would only be eight to ten hours in each town, I collected, weeks before we sailed, as many brochures and guide books with maps as I could. By their aid I worked out the aspect of every important building, planned in which order they should be photographed, and so saved myself the trouble of dashing from place to place, only to find the light always in the wrong direction! To acquaint oneself with such facts is essential; it saves so much time and disappointment.

Planning, inexhaustible patience, good weather – these are only a few points. They are, needless to say, also among the many 'Do's and Don'ts' published for the enlightenment of photographers in 1865: 'Don't be downhearted at the sight of a cloudy morning. It is frequently the sign of a fine day; and on the other hand, rarely trust a cloudless sky at nine in the morning. The chances are ten to one

C

that it will be dull by two o'clock. . . . Remember an artistic picture costs but little more trouble than a worthless one. Use your eyes well before you begin work, for though the camera is a most obedient instrument, *you* must first *see* the picture, for you cannot expect the lens to see it for you. Unless you have an inexhaustible stock of patience, stop at home.'

PATIENCE

To illustrate what patience may be required of a photographer, may I be permitted to draw once more upon my own experience. A few years ago a publisher asked me to take some photographs for a series to illustrate unexpected beauty in industrial towns. The summer and autumn of that year were exceptionally cloudy, and to fulfil this and other commissions was just a series of headaches. For weeks I listened anxiously to every weather forecast, but there seemed no chance of getting a sunny period. At last one evening the radio prophesied fine weather in the Midlands. In the next bulletin the same statement was repeated, and on phoning the Air Ministry a little later I was given the welcome news once more. Assured at last that little risk was involved in my going away, I took the midnight train to Manchester. The prospects for a sunny day seemed good in the early morning when I arrived, but it was disheartening to see how after nine o'clock the sunlight was gradually weakened by increasing mist until in the end it disappeared altogether. Implicitly trusting the various forecasts, I stayed in Manchester for five days without any improvement in the weather. Eventually I decided to try my luck in Liverpool, though heaven only knows why I thought it might be better there. Before leaving Manchester, however, I took a few photographs of views which had their charm even on a dull day, and one of them, of the River Irwell, is reproduced in Plate 27. In retrospect I am glad that I took this photograph in spite of the weather, for I probably obtained a more characteristic picture of Manchester than if I had waited for brilliant sunshine which, I am told by Mancunians, happens only at the Greek Kalends.

THE WHOLE VIEW

One of the most difficult pictures, and usually the least interesting, to make of any building or interior is the whole view; yet this is usually a necessary one, which should be supplemented by a number of detail photographs. For the whole view, the setting of the building should be well considered, for the surroundings will often help to express its function and convey an idea of its site. The inclusion of suitable foregrounds, such as an ornament which is part of the building, at once transports us into the atmosphere of the period and, pictorially speaking, gives depth to the picture.

DETAIL PHOTOGRAPHS

The value of detail photographs is still not sufficiently realised, though it had already been pointed out by the *Art Journal* in 1858 and reiterated in 1904 by Frederick H. Evans. 'It would be a good plan for the worker who desires pictures rather than views,' he wrote, 'to make at least one visit to a cathedral, and to take an 8- or a 9-inch lens, and compel himself to find subjects to suit it, and that will compose properly upon his ground glass. The lesson will be a valuable one, showing how much more charming these "bits" will be as pictures, and as souvenirs of the visit, than the usual long length views up and down and across and across.' Detail photographs help to convey a feeling of the character of the whole, or a knowledge of construction and ornamentation. Though subordinate to the whole, details often convey better the spirit of a building or bring us into more personal contact with it, than a photograph of an entire façade or interior. Master-craftsmen have spent much time and love on ornamentation which tends to be overlooked without detail photographs. (See Plate 6).

A great many of the details which I photographed had never been properly appreciated at all, often because they are situated so high or in such inaccessible positions that they cannot be clearly seen. Many of the interior photographs were taken from a 'Heathman' and from huge folding ladders, from galleries, triforiums, windowsills, organ lofts and, in one or two cases, from the High Altar itself. In cases when it was desired to obtain exterior photographs of details in high-up positions I carried the camera up to the tops of towers and mounted my tripod on roofs of houses and churches, from which a false step would have meant certain death. I learned to walk safely in rubber-soled shoes across gabled roofs, my sure-footed assistant always acting as guide and helpmate, which gave me confidence. But in a few particularly tricky places on St Paul's, where even example and confidence would not move me an inch further, I had myself roped on. On one occasion – on dizzy heights and after some considerable contemplation of the merits of the picture from beneath my black cloth – I saw to my astonishment a crowd assembled in the street, gazing up evidently in the belief that I was about to commit suicide!

PEOPLE, TRAFFIC AND FURNITURE

The reader may be struck by the complete absence of people in these photographs. My wife once jokingly called me an inhuman photographer, and she was right.

Almost right – for the human element *is* lacking in my architectural photographs! People and traffic are purposely avoided because I regard them as a distraction from the actual subject. I usually choose a moment when the road is comparatively free from traffic, or cap my lens if an obstruction comes in the way. In busy streets it is best to photograph on days when there is little traffic and one can plant the camera in the middle of the road without fear of becoming a nuisance or of being run over while considering the best viewpoint from beneath the black cloth. Parked cars or bicycles cannot be considered an embellishment to architectural photographs either, and whenever possible I ask the owner to remove his vehicle, and failing to find him I just wait. In a church interior it may sometimes be necessary to have unsightly pieces of furniture removed, such as barriers around monuments, hymn boards, or rows of chairs which obstruct the view: talking the matter over with someone in authority will usually produce full understanding of one's needs.

LIGHTING

For general views of large interiors such as cathedrals, the natural diffused lighting will best convey the character and atmosphere of the building. It would be impossible to photograph such interiors by artificial light without destroying their effect: I found, however, that artificial light may be used with advantage to supplement the natural lighting when applied to a particularly dark spot (perhaps only for a part of the exposure). The summer months are naturally the best for the photography of interiors; exposures may easily jump from half-an-hour or an hour to several hours in the winter. Lighting conditions should be carefully studied in each particular case, because much depends on the number and height of windows, the quantity of stained glass, the time of day, the colour of the stone or paint. Whether the building has a light-coloured stone or a dark wooden ceiling also makes a considerable difference in the amount of reflected light.

For the photography of architectural details and monuments I was, I believe, the first in this country to make use of floodlights. I was not only able in this way to obtain in a comparatively short time photographs which would have meant hours of exposure under normal lighting conditions or would have been completely impossible (such as details of ceilings or ornaments in dark positions), but they helped to bring out the forms more strongly than would have been possible in the diffused natural light.

In public buildings and churches the light is generally very diffused, coming from a number of directions. This results in an extraordinarily flat appearance of monuments and sculpture. Only in rare cases is a monument (by chance, or design of the artist), well placed in relation to the windows. Usually it receives all the light from one side, casting deep shadows on the other, and this unequal lighting effect can only be balanced by artificial light. Sometimes a monument may even be placed against a window, where it loses all effect and cannot be photographed by any other means than artificial light if its artistic qualities are to be brought out. The use of artificial light thus made me independent of the usually unfavourable lighting conditions in interiors.

I always had an abhorrence of the dull, uninspired photographs in books on architecture and sculpture, and realised that their *technical* shortcomings were often due to the diffused or flat lighting prevalent in most buildings. It was evident to me that real appreciation of art could only be brought about by photographs which had plasticity and which could stimulate the imagination. To this end floodlighting seemed to me essential, for *it is light which lends visual substance to form*.

It will be seen, therefore, that I arrived at this idea not so much through force of circumstance (in that a number of buildings had their windows boarded up) as by simply applying my technique of isolating details from their surroundings, which I had learned from experience in other branches of photography. In this way I could reveal unexpected beauty and visual values never realised before, at the same time emphasising through dramatic effects the structure and texture of materials. This applies equally to the photography of sculpture, for *photographing sculpture is modelling with light*.

BENVENUTO CELLINI'S EXPERIMENT

Benvenuto Cellini was probably the first artist to mention that sculpture could be endowed with unique charm and mysterious beauty by the use of artificial light, which gives quite a different effect from daylight. In his autobiography he relates a very interesting experiment in 1544. Cellini wanted to show his patron Francis I, the King of France, his silver statue of Jupiter, which he had brought for the purpose into the gallery at Fontainebleau. Unfortunately the king was prevented from coming until the evening, and Cellini feared that his work would not be seen to advantage. He therefore skilfully inserted a white waxen torch into the right hand of the statue, which was raised above its head. As soon as the King appeared Cellini lit the torch, and to his great relief and delight 'the light which fell from above made the figure seem much more beautiful than it had appeared by daylight', and the King exclaimed: 'This is by far the finest thing that has ever been seen;

and much as I delight in works of art and understand them, I could never have imagined the hundredth part of the wonder of this one.' Cellini makes no secret of the fact that a great deal of the praise showered upon him by the Court that evening was due to the novel and striking lighting effect.

GRASP OF THE ARTIST'S INTENTION

Of course, the skilful use of lighting is not the only, though a very important, factor in the photography of sculpture. Success depends equally on the photographer's ability to acquire the sculptor's faculty of seeing and thinking all round his model. The front view is usually the best if the figure is standing against a wall. If, however, the sculpture is free-standing because it is meant to be seen from all sides, it may present several good views. Whole monuments should only be photographed from the front as they are meant to be seen from that position. Details, on the other hand, may often be photographed with advantage from other viewpoints, after full consideration has been given to the particular circumstances. Whether the result is good or bad is largely dependent on the photographer's grasp of the artist's intention. Only this, and a sensitive feeling for form, will enable him to bring out the character of the artist's work. His personal attitude to the subject matters more than anything else; he has to see more in it than merely a precious but dead object. A good record is an accurate reproduction of all the technical details of a piece of sculpture, but it will betray little of the soul with which the artist has endowed his creation. The photographer must try to infuse his work with life, and in lighting he has a powerful means at his disposal for his interpretation, for photographing sculpture is modelling with light. Good lighting can enhance the sculptor's work: bad lighting can entirely destroy its effect. Shadows should fall naturally and should not be allowed to confuse the form of the sculpture. Sculptors work in a three-dimensional medium, and it must always be the photographer's chief aim to obtain depth with his lighting and re-create the three-dimensional illusion.

SMALL FIGURES AND THEIR BACKGROUND

Small figures call for a slightly different technique. They are best photographed by daylight, directed in such a way that the forms are clearly brought out. The glare of floodlights or direct sunshine is likely to destroy modelling and texture. A small beam of light from a skylight will, on the whole, be found the best form of lighting: failing this, side light which is reflected onto the other side of the sculpture by means of white cardboard gives excellent results.

Plain backgrounds of a neutral colour are the best. The very disturbing dividing line of lateral and vertical backgrounds, which is so often evident in photographs, can be avoided by using a large sheet of thin card on which the figure is placed, and which is then curved up in a concave shape behind it. The common mistake of using black or dark-coloured backgrounds for white or light-coloured sculpture should be avoided at all costs, for the immense contrast thus created 'kills' the sculpture. It has the very opposite effect of what the photographer intended. Instead of getting greater plasticity he obtains less. The sculpture does not stand out from the background but seems to be in the same plane. Sculpture needs 'air' and a feeling of space.

Small figures should be photographed from a low angle (see Plate 42a and b); looking down on them tends to give them rather a foreshortened appearance. Small models of statues for large monuments should be taken from a still lower viewpoint to produce a monumental effect.

PART III

PHOTOGRAPHIC EQUIPMENT AND PRACTICAL CONSIDERATIONS

ALTHOUGH it is probably generally recognised by now that the quality of a photograph does not depend upon the equipment used but upon the vision and technical ability of the man behind the camera, it is nevertheless important to have the most suitable equipment, for without it a photographer may be immensely handicapped in his work.

Before describing my camera, which I regard as ideal for architectural and sculptural work (and which is equally suitable for portraiture and commercial photography) may I sound a warning note – the Ideal Camera in the abstract sense does not, and perhaps never will, exist. Everyone has different ideals, and what may be ideal to me may not suit someone else. Ideal is that which is best suited to one's needs. It is, therefore, of the utmost importance to analyse one's needs, to know for what purpose one wishes to use a camera, and whether it can perform the functions expected of it. It may, for instance, seem obvious that a field camera is not suitable for Press work, but it may appear less obvious that square reflex or miniature cameras are totally unsuitable for architectural and sculptural photography. Architectural photographs taken with such cameras are usually easily detectible by their inclination of vertical lines, and though this fault can be corrected in the enlarger, rectification of converging lines by tilting the easel of the enlarger is an irksome and time-wasting procedure. Andreas Feininger states that 'about six out of every ten negatives' which he took for his book *New York* were corrected in this way; yet this should remain a necessity, justified in Feininger's special case, and not made a virtue. Feininger's intention was to give what he called 'The portrait of a city', not to photograph its architecture. Naturally it is impossible to catch the pulsating life of a town with a bulky view camera.

THE CAMERA

Almost any kind of plate or view camera 9 x 12 cm. or larger can be used. For such exacting work ground glass focusing is of vital importance. By its aid the composition can be studied and the effect of lenses of varying focal length properly judged; at the same time an accurate idea of the depth of field when stopping down is gained. I strongly recommend the square form of camera with reversible back, i.e. in which only the ground glass need be turned if a change-over from the vertical to the horizontal view is desired. It must have a good rising front, an interchangeable lens panel, and at least double, preferably triple, bellows extension to allow the use of lenses of long focal length. To facilitate work with such lenses, the back of the camera should be provided with rack focusing, and this will also be found of great advantage when using a wide-angle lens. Hand cameras with fixed camera backs must have a falling baseboard to avoid its inclusion with a wide-angle lens, and this in turn necessitates a tilting lens board.

My camera is a 'Kuhn-Stegemann', size 9 × 12 cm, resembling in appearance the new American Grover monorail camera, which is based on it and may be known to the reader. An unusual feature of the camera is that its front and back slide on a prism-shaped rod instead of the usual camera base. It is square in construction and has a 20-inch bellows extension – more than triple, assuming a normal focal length of 6 inches for this plate size. I use a whole range of lenses, from $3\frac{1}{8}$-inch wide-angle to 14-inch, each set in its own lens panel, which allows me rapidly to change over from one to another. The camera is equipped with a good rising and falling front and a vertical and lateral swing-back of up to 30°; the latter, however, I have never used.*

LENSES

Without a wide-angle lens the architectural photographer cannot work, but its use should be restricted to conditions absolutely necessitating it. Generally, a short focal length (i.e. equal to the longer side of the plate) will be found sufficient for interior views and general outdoor work. The use of longer focal lengths may often be impossible because of limited space, though one should move the camera as far away as possible from a building or interior, to avoid any false perspective. It is a fallacy that distortion of perspective is due to the use of a wide-angle lens. Distortion is usually due to too short a distance of camera from object. For detail photographs lenses of long focal length are required.

Town views or more distant architectural exterior views can be satisfactorily taken with a reflex or miniature camera.

---

* In my article "Design of Equipment", *Process Engravers Monthly*, May 1944, the camera is described in greater detail

TRIPOD AND OTHER ACCESSORIES

A firm tripod which will withstand vibration from wind is a necessity. The 'Linhof' with which I work can be extended up to 6 foot (it measures 2 foot 6 inches when closed). It has a large ball and socket head which can be tilted and locked in any position up to 90°. This device allows complete freedom in photographing at an angle, without necessitating adjusting the legs of the tripod. The legs are fitted with quickly interchangeable metal spikes for outdoor, or rubber tips for indoor work. This tripod has in addition a locking device so that the legs stay put at any given angle, which is a great help when adjusting the camera to a chosen viewpoint. This device also guards against slipping on polished floors. However, placing the tripod on a small rug will answer the purpose equally well.

To protect the lens against stray light I regard the use of a *lens hood* as an absolute necessity.

A *spirit level* will also be found useful, but the marking of one or two vertical and horizontal lines near the edge of the ground glass and a cross indicating its centre will be found a simpler and equally good arrangement.

PLATES

Plates should be panchromatic, of medium speed, and of soft gradation. Very fast plates have not such a good colour balance, and are in any case not necessary because the nature of the work calls on the whole for long exposures. Soft gradation is required because in this branch of photography one has often to deal with subjects of great light contrast. The plates should be backed against halation, which is the bugbear of interior work.

FILTERS

Filters are rarely needed in architectural or sculptural photography, though sometimes it may be desirable to increase the tone contrast when a white or light-coloured building or architectural detail is photographed against a pale sky. To bring out detail in dark oak carving, or marquetry, a red filter may occasionally be required.

EXPOSURE METER

I use no exposure meter – experience alone guides me, and only on the rarest occasions do I feel prompted by uncertainty to make two negatives of the same subject. I arrived at this method largely by standardisation: I have found that particular negative and positive materials and certain developers are best suited to the kind of work I do, and I stick to them. I have also learned to standardise my stops, and to judge the intensity of light which falls on the ground glass after I have stopped down. I usually stop down to F.36 in order to obtain sufficient depth of field with lenses of long focal length, but with the wide-angle lens the smallest stop only is used, in order to ensure first-rate definition right to the corners, for it has the extraordinary range of field of 105°.

Any one who is not yet able to judge an exposure by experience will find that an electric exposure meter will give fairly accurate readings for outdoor work, but cannot be relied upon for dim interiors. Under poor light conditions I strongly recommend the use of a visual exposure meter, provided that one allows one's eyes to adjust themselves to the prevailing light before making the reading.

Exposures for interiors should always be on the long rather than on the short side, and it is advisable to treble or quadruple the exposure time recorded by the meter. If one does misjudge the exposure, and development does not yield a good negative, one should throw it away and start afresh. In the long run it saves time. To make do with a poor negative is bad policy and causes far more annoyance.

LIGHTING

I generally use two 500-watt floodlights, and occasionally a third floodlight to light up very large or dark interiors. By moving this supplementary light beam about, those areas which are not illuminated equally by the static floodlights or the natural lighting are strengthened. In photographing ceilings or reliefs the light should be placed at an angle so as to bring out the detail in relief. In lighting up monuments the lights will usually have to be placed on tables or otherwise raised well above the ground so as to give a natural effect as if the light were coming from a high window.

When I was photographing monuments in Westminster Abbey, some of which are situated 20 feet or more above the ground, my assistant suggested attaching one light to a long pole which he then held in position. The other light was fixed lower down to produce an even lighting effect, i.e., to make the shadows cast by the higher light translucent. Even with this method it was sometimes necessary to illuminate from below a detail which remained out of our reach, as can be seen, for instance, in the Grabe and Händel monuments (Plates 43 and 58). If this is done carefully the interpretation will not suffer: in fact, as both these monuments are rather theatrical in style, lighting from below intensified their dramatic effect.

FLASHLIGHT

The use of flashlight for interiors or sculpture is to be strongly discouraged. Flashlight tends to be harsh and is unmanageable; one cannot foresee how the light will fall upon the subject at the precise moment of making the exposure. It was clear to me that it would never serve my purpose, even if used with floodlight technique; for bringing out a relief or modulation of a figure or head depends on dead accuracy in placing the lights – moving the light an inch either way from the right position may completely ruin the effect. In any case floodlight is often required for general illumination to do the preliminary work before the exposure.

WORKING FROM LADDERS

It goes without saying that the photographer and camera have to be raised as far as possible to the height of the monument or detail to be photographed. Sometimes it is sufficient to set up the tripod on a table and stand on a chair behind it, but in Westminster Abbey and at the British Museum I had to work to a large extent from a 'Heathman' which could be extended to various heights. On this I was wheeled about by an assistant, having firmly planted my camera and myself on the platform. In St Paul's, where no 'Heathman' was available, I worked from the top of a heavy 20-foot folding ladder, which needed four men to shift. As it was impossible to fix the tripod with any degree of security to the ladder some other means had to be devised. The problem was eventually solved in the following way, which is strongly recommended whenever photographs have to be taken from ladders.

I bought a reflector of the type used to light up goods in shop windows. These lights have a bracket with two screw holes for fixing it to the ceiling. The bracket can be quickly screwed on to any ladder which has a flat top. I also bought a separate ball and socket head which fitted on to the thread of the bracket. By this method it was found an easy matter to fix the camera on top of any ladder, the ball and socket head allowing the camera the same freedom of movement as when it is fixed to the tripod. Furthermore, it was quite safe to move the ladder with the camera in position.

When the exposure was of a comparatively short duration (5 to 10 minutes) I remained standing on the ladder behind the camera, making as little movement as possible. Should the exposure be longer, it is preferable to uncap the lens and descend the ladder. The small shake caused by the descent, and ascent to end the exposure, will have no effect upon the sharpness of the picture. Similarly, the movement of people in and out of an interior during a long exposure will make no impression upon the plate. If any uncertainty is felt, the best plan may be to switch off the lights before opening the shutter, and similarly before climbing up to end the exposure.

As the National Buildings Record scheme had the full support of the Ministry of Works and Buildings, one and sometimes two assistants were usually provided to help me – though sometimes I had to fight hard to convince the authorities that without such aid most of my work would be impossible. My assistants were always members of the maintenance staff of the building in question, laid the necessary cables, made the electric contacts, knew the position of fuse boxes etc, and held the lights in position. In order to be undisturbed by the public and to prevent any one falling over the cables, an area was always roped off round the monument on which I was working.

When working without such assistance, the importance of making extensive preparations cannot be over-emphasised. I have sometimes spent a whole day in search of ladders or backgrounds. *Without taking such trouble a photographer cannot expect to obtain the best results.*

ELECTRICITY SUPPLY

It is also important to ascertain the position of light points, and the size of light or power plugs required, for as long as there is no standardisation in electrical fittings in this country, without such preliminary knowledge the photographer may have to carry with him two sets of light bulbs (for 110 and 220 volts) and at least eight different kinds of plug for each light contact. Moreover, valuable time is lost in changing the plugs over on the site. It is recommendable to acquaint oneself with the position of fuse boxes and to carry in one's bag a certain amount of fuse wire, for fusing is the most common mishap.

For those who wish to work with electric light it is essential to know what load an installation will safely carry; for one cannot plug in as many floodlights as one likes without dangerously overloading it. The wattage one can safely use can by worked out by multiplying the voltage by the amperage – both of which are indicated on electric meters, e.g. 220 volt × 6 amp. = 1320 watts. In this case one can use two 500-watt lamps. If the voltage is only 110 and the amperage 5, 110 volt × 5 amp. = 550 watts. In this case only one 500-watt lamp or two 250-watt lamps may be used.

Electricity supply can be a great problem on occasion. I was once asked to photograph the oldest wall paintings in Britain for reproduction in a book.* These paintings, in two little Sussex country churches, are fading fast, and in the absence

* *Twelfth Century Paintings at Hardham and Clayton*, with an introductory essay by Clive Bell

of a photographic record there had been much controversy regarding the interpretation of some of them.

The difficulties with which the publishers and I were faced were considerable, for on account of the great height of the paintings, steel scaffolding had to be erected throughout the interior of both churches. In addition, one of the churches had only oil lamps for illumination and there was no house in the neighbourhood which had electricity laid on. There remained only one possibility – to obtain a dynamo and generate electricity ourselves. After a long search we secured one. The light obtained from it was very uneven and my floodlights burned only at about half strength, but after some test pictures I found the correct exposure time.

DARKROOM WORK

My negatives are developed in glycine, which is a slower and therefore more controllable developer than metol-hydroquinone and gives softer negatives. I practise dish development exclusively, because photographs taken under difficult lighting conditions require individual treatment to obtain first-rate results. If a negative is not perfect, it is thrown away. I never intensify, but I usually develop to a slightly greater density than required; for in order to obtain increased brilliance with soft gradation negative material it is advisable to reduce the plates, wholly or partially, in potassium ferricyanide, which has the additional advantage of producing a more or less uniform density similar to that obtained with miniature films by time development.

It has probably become clear from the foregoing that I do not select a portion of the negative for enlargement; details have been specially photographed. To have to trim the image originally photographed is, I think, an admission of failure. The important thing is to be able to recognise the significance of a subject before making the exposure and not afterwards.

To get the most out of the negatives I print only on glossy paper, which gives greater brilliance and detail than a matt or semi-matt surface. Except for exhibition purposes the 9 × 12 cm negatives are enlarged to wholeplate size only. They are entirely unretouched – only dust-spotted – and all I do is to shade off or after-expose parts as necessary to extend the tone-scale, for it is a well-known fact that the tone-scale of the positive emulsion corresponds only to about one-tenth of that of the negative emulsion.

I do all my own copying and enlarging, believing that only the man who took the photograph is able to re-visualise the tone-values which he saw at the time of exposure.

PLATES 1—32

1. ST PAUL'S CATHEDRAL FROM THE EAST

2. ST PAUL'S CATHEDRAL. SOUTH-WEST TOWER

3. ST PAUL'S CATHEDRAL. DETAIL OF SOUTH-WEST TOWER—UPPER GALLERY

4. ST PAUL'S CATHEDRAL. CIRCULAR STAIRCASE, LOOKING UP

5. ST PAUL'S CATHEDRAL, CIRCULAR STAIRCASE, LOOKING DOWN

6. ST PAUL'S CATHEDRAL. DECORATIVE SHELL WINDOW

7. ST PAUL'S CATHEDRAL. CORINTHIAN CAPITAL IN DRUM GALLERY, AND SOUTH-WEST TOWER

8. HIGHGATE CEMETERY. ENTRANCE TO THE 'EGYPTIAN' AVENUE

9. HIGHGATE CEMETERY. THE CIRCULAR ROAD WITH CATACOMBS ON EITHER SIDE

10. ASHBURNHAM HOUSE, STAIRCASE

11. LIVERPOOL TOWN HALL. STAIRCASE WELL AND DOME

12. THE CARYATIDS, SOUTH PORTICO OF THE ERECHTHEION ON THE ACROPOLIS, ATHENS

13. THE PROPYLAEA, ACROPOLIS, ATHENS, DETAIL OF IONIC COLUMN

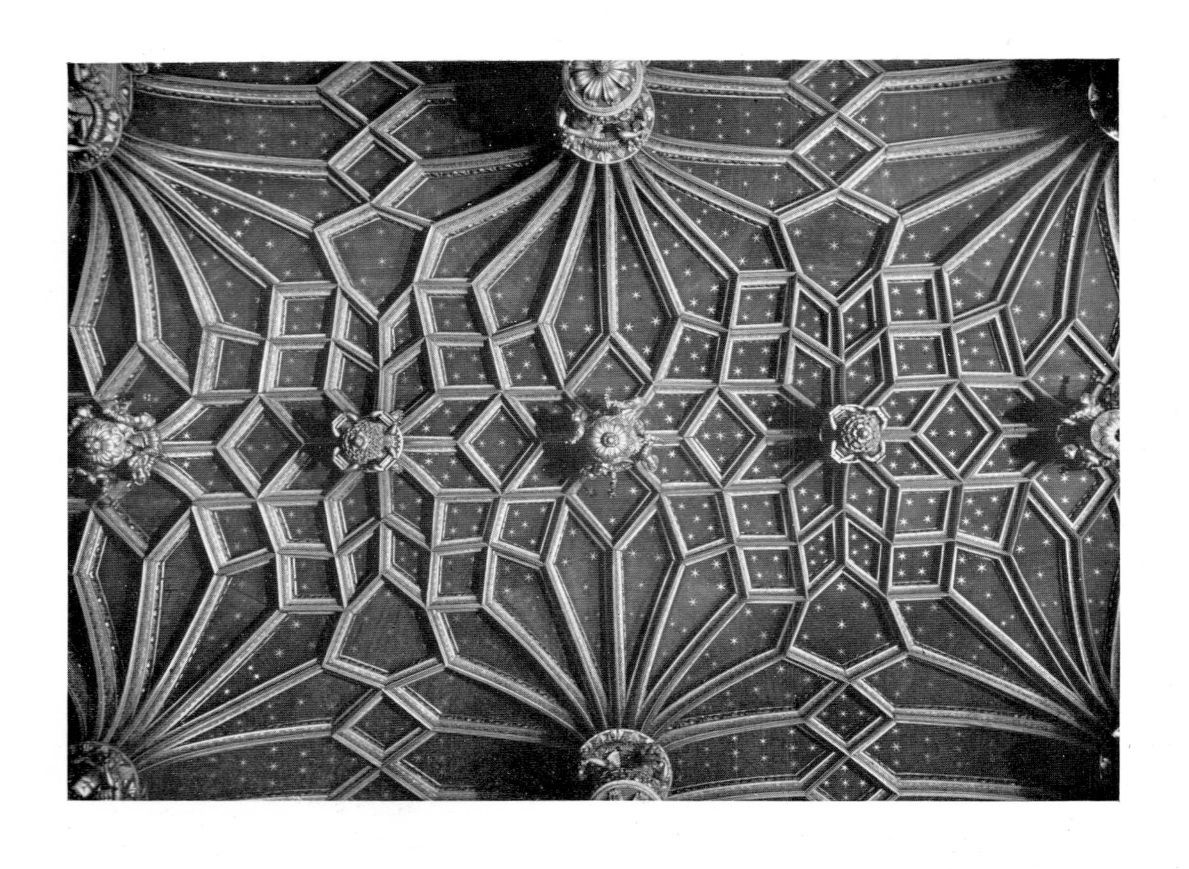

14. HAMPTON COURT PALACE, CHAPEL ROYAL. WHOLE CEILING

15. HAMPTON COURT PALACE, CHAPEL ROYAL. DETAIL OF CEILING

16. NATIONAL MUSEUM, MUNICH. GOTHIC ROOM

31. OXFORD. CHRIST CHURCH. APPROACH TO PECKWATER QUAD

32. THE PICTURESQUE - BY ENEMY ACTION

NOTES TO THE PLATES ON ARCHITECTURE

Plate 1. ST PAUL'S CATHEDRAL *from the east*

The imposing dome of St Paul's is the one outstanding feature of London's skyline, dwarfing all other buildings.

Wren's masterpiece, which occupied him for thirty-five years, was completed in 1710. It is the fourth largest cathedral in the world: only those of Rome, Seville and Milan are larger.

St Paul's has been photographed countless times, but this is one of the first, if not the first, photograph to show the whole majestic structure of the cathedral from the east – a vista opened up by German bombs. I climbed the tower of St Mary-le-Bow early one morning, so as to catch the sunlight striking the apse.

Plate 2. ST PAUL'S CATHEDRAL *South-west tower*

The south-west or clock tower houses 'Great Paul', Britain's largest bell.

The west towers are perhaps St Paul's most attractive features, for in them as Dr Margaret Whinney points out in her Cathedral book *St Paul's*: 'Wren exploits to a greater degree than anywhere else in his work those baroque qualities of a play of curve against curve, of broken silhouettes, of ornaments designed to lead the eye from one stage to the next, and above all, of motives arranged to give the maximum contrast of light and shade'. The view was obtained from the drum gallery which runs round the base of the dome, as the wonderful rhythm could be better appreciated from this position than from street level. The clear atmosphere of the summer morning afforded a wide view over London. The balloons dotted about in the sky are part of the balloon barrage during the 1939–45 war.

Plate 3. ST PAUL'S CATHEDRAL. *Detail of south-west tower – upper gallery*

The lovely arcading with its baroque vases affords a most attractive light and shade effect. Good timing and freedom from giddiness were necessary, for this gallery can only be reached by climbing a repair workers' ladder which runs inside the tower and past one of the bells. The ledge is only two or at the most three feet wide, but the presence and watchful eye of an assistant reassured me when contemplating this view from underneath the black cloth.

Plates 4 and 5. ST PAUL'S CATHEDRAL. *Circular staircase, looking up and looking down*

Built in 1705, the splendid circular staircase which runs inside the south-west tower up to the triforium and to the Cathedral library was originally intended by Wren – so I have been told – to lead to an observatory which Charles II gave him permission to build in the tower, but Parliament withheld consent. The magnificence of the staircase is overpowering.

The regular 'snail' pattern of Plate 4 was obtained by lying with the camera in the centre of the floor.

For a short time during the exposure one 500-watt lamp was used to illuminate the underside of the steps.

Plate 5 affords quite a different view of the staircase, a more unusual one, in my opinion. The irregular pattern was obtained through distortion due to the fact that it was not (and could not be) photographed from the centre. The view was taken from the balcony leading to the triforium. Camera and tripod were firmly fixed projecting a few feet over the staircase well, and I myself was held out by an assistant, in order to arrange and focus the picture on the ground glass.

Plate 6. ST PAUL'S CATHEDRAL. *Decorative Shell Window*

The whole of the south side of St Paul's Cathedral was photographed section by section in over a hundred detail photographs, including the fine decorative work which, though small in scale and restrained in character, was executed with great skill by Wren's master-craftsmen, but is hardly visible at street level. Naturally a fresh viewpoint had to be selected from the surrounding buildings for nearly every picture. Some of the carved panels under the windows were photographed from the top of a ladder.

Plate 7. ST PAUL'S CATHEDRAL. *Corinthian capital in drum gallery, and south-west tower*

I crammed myself and the camera into a little niche where pigeons and starlings roost, and obtained a picture of a superb detail from an angle at which few human eyes have seen it before. Comparing this picture with Plate 2, the picturesque effect obtained through the introduction of the capital will perhaps be more readily appreciated.

The technical data may be of interest in this case. Working with a plate of 25° Scheiner I gave an exposure of 20 seconds at F.32. An exposure of this length for an outdoor picture may surprise the reader. Though there was only weak sunshine that morning, the light contrast between the gleaming white tower and the almost black parts of the capital where it is sheltered from the weather, and in the shade, was quite extraordinary.

The plate was developed in a very diluted solution, but even then the contrast appeared too great at first and had to be diminished by partial reduction with potassium ferricyanide.

Plate 8. HIGHGATE CEMETERY. *Entrance to the 'Egyptian' avenue*

The grounds of this cemetery were laid out about 1838 by the architect S. Geary in collaboration with a landscape gardener, D. Ramsay. Two curious features, known to few Londoners, are the strange 'Egyptian' avenue and the catacombs, the only ones in England.

The entrance to the avenue, flanked by two pairs of 'Egyptian' double columns and obelisks, and overshadowed by a drooping poplar tree, is one of the most attractive bits of landscape gardening in London. On each side of the avenue are eight sepulchres furnished with stone shelves for the coffins. The avenue terminates in a sunken circular road about five hundred feet in circumference, flanked by sepulchres similar to those in the avenue. The inner circle thus forms a large 'building', with a flat roof from the midst of which rises a beautiful Cedar of Lebanon. The whole resembles a miniature city of tombs in the Egyptian style of architecture, while the Neo-Gothic church of St Michael on the summit of the hill forms a curious contrast in the background.

Plate 9. HIGHGATE CEMETERY. *The circular road with catacombs on either side*

The tombs on the right are of later date than the 'Egyptian' ones on the left.

Plate 10. ASHBURNHAM HOUSE. *Staircase*

Ashburnham House was built about 1640 by Inigo Jones. The superb staircase with its fine panelling and fluted columns is a masterpiece, unfortunately not widely known. Mr Sacheverell Sitwell said of it that 'It would be no exaggeration, remembering the staircases in Italian palaces, to say that this, within its modest dimensions, is as fine as any'.

Ashburnham House is named after Colonel William Ashburnham, a noted Royalist and personal friend of Charles II, who occupied it in 1662. In 1882 it was incorporated in the Westminster School buildings and housed its library until 1940. It was the 'Churchill Club' from May 1943 to December 1945, when the premises reverted to the School.

The view gives an impression of the structure of the staircase, with the exception of its beautiful dome, and was taken from the utmost corner of the bend of the stairs. The inclusion of part of the column and its base on the extreme left is an important feature, for without it the design and spacing of the staircase would be unintelligible. The lighting was natural, coming from the domed roof and from a window behind the camera. The portrait on the opposite wall showed a disturbing reflection seen from this position. The difficulty was overcome by altering the angle of the picture slightly by inserting a wedge behind one corner of the frame.

Plate 11. LIVERPOOL TOWN HALL. *Staircase well and dome*

The Town Hall is Liverpool's second oldest public building, and was erected in the Palladian style by John Wood, the architect of Bath, in 1749-54, the dome being added by James Wyatt in 1795.

The photograph was taken from the stairs looking straight up into the dome, care being taken to include the whole of the square cornice at the top of the staircase well, in order to make the construction clear. To show detail in the coffered ceiling of the dome, and the four painted lunettes, two floodlights were used during the exposure. No-one was allowed to go up or down the stairs during this time, in order not to shake the carpet on which the camera stood, and I am afraid this caused a little excitement among the officials, for I extended my exposure, originally timed for an hour, by another thirty minutes and only finished just before the Lord Mayor was due to sit down to an official luncheon.

Plate 12. THE CARYATIDS. *South portico of the Erechtheion on the Acropolis, Athens*

These figures of Athenian maidens serve as an architectural support of the architrave of the south portico of the temple known as the Erechtheion, which was completed about 410 B.C. The almost faceless Caryatids are timeless in majesty. For centuries they have been admired for their easy grace combined with strength and solidity as architectural features.

Female figures used in this way in architecture were in later antiquity called Caryatids, which means women of Caryæ, a town in Arcadia. The Greeks merely called them 'Kores' which means maidens. The third Caryatid from the left is a nineteenth century reproduction: the original can be seen in the British Museum.

A copy of the portico was incorporated in St Pancras Church, Euston Road, rebuilt by William and Henry Inwood in 1822.

Plate 13. THE PROPYLÆA, ACROPOLIS, ATHENS. *Detail of Ionic column*

The Propylæa is the entrance to the Acropolis, and this picture includes the only remnant of the coffered ceiling of the inner hall, supported by an Ionic column.

Angle shots should only be resorted to in rare instances like this when the nature of the subject justifies it. This sort of view suggests height and gives exactly the effect which the eye sees when looking up. One so often sees meaningless angle shots, whole buildings tipped sideways apparently in the vain hope of making the photograph more interesting. What can be done in a detail photograph when there is a clear purpose behind it, must be regarded as a failure when attempted with a whole building.

Plate 14. HAMPTON COURT PALACE, CHAPEL ROYAL. *Whole ceiling*

Owing to the poor lighting conditions in the Chapel, the famous Tudor ceiling had never been photographed before.

The illustration shows practically the whole ceiling, i.e. as much as I could get in with the wide-angle lens. Two stationary floodlights were so placed at an angle to the ceiling as to make the pattern effect intelligible by casting a small shadow behind each rib and pendant. A third floodlight was kept constantly moving, to strengthen those parts which were not completely covered by the beams of the static lights. The Chaplain was so impressed by the effects of my lighting that he had floodlighting installed soon afterwards, 'inspired by what I saw when you were taking the photographs', as he wrote to me.

Plate 15. HAMPTON COURT PALACE, CHAPEL ROYAL. *Detail of ceiling*

A vertical view of a ceiling is only one way of looking at it and photographing it: in this case quite indispensable because of the fine pattern. Very often, however, a diagonal view will give a better impression when the important issue is not pattern but shape or detail, whether stucco or carved.

This close-up was taken after a diagonal view of the whole ceiling had been obtained. The pendants, which look like bosses in the vertical view, are now brought out in their true depth, and the shape of the ceiling and the elaborate carving on ribs and pendants are revealed in their full beauty.

Plate 16. NATIONAL MUSEUM, MUNICH. *Gothic Room*

The National Museum at Munich contains one of the best collections of German fine and applied art. The present building, designed by Gabriel v. Seidl, was erected in 1900. The interior decoration is chiefly by Rudolph v. Seitz, each room in the historical section reflecting in its fitting up the period to which its contents belong.

This against-the-light picture was taken without the assistance of artificial light. The long exposure necessary to obtain sufficient detail in the dark parts of the interior caused the window to be greatly over-exposed. I gave four times the exposure which I read off from an optical exposure meter to produce a soft negative, and though the plate was most carefully developed in a very slow developer, the contrast was still so great that no detail could be obtained in the stained glass panels when printing it. To reduce the contrast the negative was bleached and re-developed, but not quite to the previous density.

Plate 17. INTERIOR OF A BAVARIAN BAROQUE CHURCH

This, my first architectural photograph (1935), is still one of my favourites. The subject is the south aisle of the Church of the Holy Ghost in Munich, rebuilt in late baroque style in 1724-30 by the brothers Asam. The sunlight from the windows on the right highlights the pilasters, making each stand out separately, thus greatly enhancing the perspective effect of the view. Through the inclusion of part of the wrought iron gate – a very picturesque feature often found in South German and Austrian baroque and rococo churches – an impression of depth is achieved, the black metal forming a pleasing contrast to the white-washed pillars.

The photograph was taken with an ordinary 9 × 12 cm plate camera fitted with a 13.5 cm lens, which shows that it is not always essential to take interior photographs with a wide-angle lens. Indeed, a much truer effect is achieved in interiors by avoiding the wide-angle lens whenever possible, as such a lens will nearly always give a disturbingly exaggerated perspective.

Plate 18. HAMPTON COURT PALACE. *The Great Hall, fan vaulted ceiling over dais*

The truly magnificent Great Hall was built by Henry VIII to replace the more modest hall of Cardinal Wolsey's palace. It was begun in 1531 and finished five years later. This beautiful fan vaulted ceiling is over the dais, which is raised one step above the floor of the main hall and lighted by a bay window. Here the king used to dine with his favourites, while the rest of the company sat at long tables ranged down each side of the Great Hall.

As previously pointed out, a ceiling, the important feature of which is its design and not its decoration, should be photographed vertically and complete to render intelligible the regularity or irregularity of the pattern.

Plate 19a. ROYAL NAVAL COLLEGE CHAPEL, GREENWICH. *Ceiling niche, underside of gallery*

Here my task consisted not only in bringing out the rich decoration but also the form, i.e. to make clear the separation of planes, the horizontal one consisting of the underside of the gallery with the cove which joins on to the vertical plane consisting of the plaque and the garlands over the blacked-out window and the arch connecting the two pilasters. Enough was included of the gallery brackets and the pilasters right and left to make the whole setting understandable.

Perhaps the least known among the many historic features at Greenwich is the Chapel, the interior of which was rebuilt by James ('Athenian') Stuart between 1779 and 1789 after a fire. James Stuart had visited Athens and was co-author, with Revett, of *The Antiquities of Athens*.

The interior contains an abundance of classical stucco ornamentation, of which this plate depicts an exceptionally fine example over a window recess underneath the gallery.

Plate 19b. ROYAL NAVAL COLLEGE CHAPEL, GREENWICH. *Detail of ornament on gallery*

This is a detail of the exquisite ornamentation which runs along the whole length of the gallery. The upper part of the ornament shows what is commonly called the egg and tongue motif, while the lower part contains the honeysuckle design.

The bold alternation of light and shade, together with the harmonious succession of curves which is implicit in the floral forms, makes an exquisite pattern in black and white. I used artificial light, for the ornament appeared very flat, being opposite a row of windows.

Plate 20a. 10 DOWNING STREET. *Mantelpiece*

The elegant marble mantelpiece in the drawing-room is by William Kent, the brilliant early eighteenth century architect and designer. The side light from the nearby window brings out the carving as well as could be desired, but one floodlight had to be used for part of the exposure to light up the grate, as the fireplace would otherwise have appeared as an unsightly black hole.

Plate 20b. HAMPTON COURT PALACE. *Fire-back*

Antique fireplaces are often fitted with cast-iron fire-backs of beautiful design. The one shown in the illustration is fixed in the fireplace of King William III's Writing Closet.

It will be evident from their position and material that these fire-backs cannot be photographed in daylight. However, due to the small size of the fireplace-opening, direct artificial light cannot be used with advantage either, for a fire-back will reflect like a mirror, without showing the design at all. The method I used came to me by accident. I was standing meditating in front of one of these fireplaces when my assistant jokingly turned the reflector on me for a moment, and that moment brought a revelation, for the light reflected from my white overall on to the fireplace lit up the design more beautifully than I could ever have imagined, and all the firebacks in the Palace were subsequently photographed in this way, hanging white material over a chair.

Plate 21. DOMESTIC INTERIOR

Interiors of homes must look natural, though it will nearly always be necessary to re-arrange or remove some of the furniture to obtain a satisfactory effect in a photograph. In this case the best position was the view from the doorway in the extreme right-hand corner, and this would have brought the table and chairs too far to the left if they had remained in the actual centre of the room. To counteract the wide-angle effect, they were moved at least two feet to the right and now appear centred to the fireplace. The chair in the right-hand bottom corner (of which part of the seat can be seen) was not left there by mistake, but because it added a feeling of space.

Natural lighting gives a much more pleasing effect to the interior of a room than artificial light, when it can be used, though the most practical method will often be to have both unobtrusively combined. Owing to the enormous light contrast when photographing against windows, and the difficulty of obtaining detail in them, a recommendable trick is to draw the blinds or curtains and to make the exposure by artificial light for nine-tenths of its duration. For the last one-tenth of the exposure the lights are switched off, the windows uncovered, and the result will give a very clear window with no trace of the curtains unless they hang down far below the windowsill. The lighting will appear very natural, the artificial light being almost completely counteracted by the strong daylight streaming in, and thus the 'window problem' is satisfactorily solved.

In the interior illustrated, the play of light and shade gives a natural and attractive effect to the room. The second window (not seen in the photograph) is indicated by the sunshine on the carpet.

When photographing interiors, care should be taken that pictures, polished furniture and mirrors do not pick up the reflection of the floodlights.

Plate 22. BROOKS' CLUB. *Staircase*

During the eighteenth century Brooks' (founded in 1764) was the leading Whig Club. William Pitt the Younger and Charles James Fox were both members.

The photograph shows an arch in the staircase well at the first floor level, with a bust of William Pitt, and was taken from the opposite side of the landing.

Normally the staircase well would be lit up by its domed glass roof, but this having been boarded up, I had to resort to artificial light. Three 500-watt lamps were used, one lighting up the bust and the lower part of the staircase well, another directed upwards to bring out the decoration on the cornice and to light up the upper part of the staircase well, and the third placed behind the wall on the left-hand side to illuminate the other staircase leading to the second floor.

Plate 23. ASHBURNHAM HOUSE. *Door leading to drawing-room (see also Plate 10)*

This exceedingly beautiful door only needed to be photographed by natural light. I considered the side view, in this case, more picturesque than the orthodox front view.

Plate 24a. HAMPTON COURT PALACE. *King's Great Staircase*

One of the most splendid staircases in England, designed by Wren as the principal approach to William III's state rooms. The walls and ceiling were painted as one great composition by Antonio Verrio, an Italian, about 1700. Verrio's pretentious and gaudy style triumphed in the reigns of Charles II, James II, William and Mary, and Anne.

The illustration shows the south wall on which are depicted Mercury dictating to Julian the Apostate, and above the door (which, like the bust over it, is not painted but real), a Roman funeral pyre. The realistic effect of the columns and pilasters is remarkable. The wrought iron balustrading is by Tijou.

In order to enable me to take this photograph (one out of a series of twenty-five of the staircase paintings), the Ministry of Works erected a scaffolding over the lower part of the staircase, to raise me to the level of the upper part.

The daylight coming from the window on the right was balanced by the light from two 1000-watt reflectors, mainly directed towards the left-hand upper corner and the right-hand bottom corner of the wall. In addition I spot-lighted the darker parts of the painting with the light beam of an ordinary 500-watt Nitraphotlamp.

Photographing painted ceilings or walls quite often falls to the task of an architectural photographer, and at Hampton Court they formed the most important part of my programme, for they had not been photographed before.

The light problem usually presented the greatest difficulty, for daylight streaming in through windows has a tendency to produce a patchy effect. Whenever possible I recommend shutting out the daylight altogether and resorting to artificial light only. This is easier than balancing the two lights to obtain an even effect.

Ceilings must be photographed straight up from the dead centre with a wide-angle lens, and from as low a position as the tripod will allow, in order to include as much as possible. For detail photographs a lens of long focal length should be used, and the camera centred below the detail.

Plate 24b. HAMPTON COURT PALACE, THE QUEEN'S STAIRCASE. *Detail*

The balustrading of the Queen's Staircase, as of the King's Staircase, is by Jean Tijou, a Huguenot who settled in England and, with Grinling Gibbons the woodcarver and Francis Bird the sculptor, forms a triad of craftsmen of genius who collaborated with Wren in a number of projects. Tijou introduced new working methods, and at Hampton Court and St Paul's we can see his finest work.

Wrought iron can be photographed either as a silhouette against a light background as in this case (indirect lighting), or by strong side light against a dark background (direct lighting). Which of the two methods is chosen depends on the kind of wrought iron work; the main thing is to make it stand out from the background. If its importance lies in design and shape, it should be indirectly lit; if the main interest lies in detail, direct lighting is preferable. Naturally, if the wrought iron work is close in front of a wall, (or very far away from it), there is no other choice but direct lighting. Generally speaking, indirect lighting gives a greater sense of space and depth. In taking this photograph two floodlights were directed on the staircase wall which runs at right-angles to the wrought iron work.

So far we have been considering chiefly close-ups of architecture, whether exterior or interior. But this book would hardly be complete without a few general views, which, though more common than the close-ups first introduced by me on a large scale, will give me occasion to stress some points which do not receive enough attention from photographers.

Plate 25. LIVERPOOL

If I were asked to take one characteristic view of Liverpool, typical of that city in all its aspects, I would choose this view again. To me the mention of Liverpool conjures up mist and Victorianism. Both are always constantly in evidence, whenever you stay in that city and wherever you go. The Victorian lamp-posts, the equestrian statue of Queen Victoria, the Wellington monument, the Neo-Classical public buildings almost without exception erected in the Victorian era, all these have been concentrated into this picture.

Plate 26. BRISTOL CANAL

Bristol still offers many fine views in spite of heavy air-raid damage. One of the most attractive is no doubt down by the Canal – a scene which might have inspired Canaletto.

This is one of the few pictures in which I found all the conditions just right when I passed by. I had only to take it.

Plate 27. MANCHESTER. *The River Irwell*

Here is the essence of Manchester, the most attractive view I could find there, and, I believe, also the most characteristic. (*See page* 34).

Plate 28. EDINBURGH. *View from Calton Hill*

The view of this beautiful city, 'The Athens of the North', as the inhabitants proudly call it, from Calton Hill is world-famous.

Generally speaking, wide town views are artistically uninteresting and often unavoidably reminiscent of picture postcards. Wishing to give an impression of the city rather than a topographical view, I decided on evening light, and the rising smoke which it shows up so well certainly creates atmosphere. To represent 'Modern Athens' without a Neo-Hellenic feature would be a poor interpretation, so I included the little monument erected in memory of Dugald Stewart, which was no doubt inspired by the monument to Lysicrates in Athens.

Plate 29. TRINITY COLLEGE CHAPEL, OXFORD

Oxford offers a wealth of picturesque effects which always surprise one afresh and reveal new and unexpected delights. A view through a dark doorway, so obviously 'picturesque', may seem a hackneyed theme, yet walking through colleges in Oxford is one long series of such views through doorways, and pictorially to avoid them would be to ignore a characteristic feature of the town. To me the broad view of Trinity College Chapel (by Wren, possibly in collaboration with Dean Aldrich, completed 1694) from the south side, with its long stretch of garden, seemed uninteresting compared with this charming detail of its tower seen from the passage to the Second Quadrangle.

Plate 30. OXFORD. CHRIST CHURCH. *Approach to Peckwater Quad*

On the right towers the Library, its flaking stonework contrasting with the smooth elegance of the Peckwater Building on the left.

Plate 31. OXFORD. CHRIST CHURCH. *Peckwater Quad*

Though a strong side light is the best form of lighting for exterior architecture because it brings out prominently the structure and texture of the building (see Plate 30), in exceptional cases a strong relief effect may also be obtained indirectly, i.e. not on the façade itself through the play of sunlight, but by throwing the whole building into relief by waiting until adjoining buildings are in the shadow. Orthodox lighting would in this picture have cast a long shadow from an adjoining building on to the Palladian façade, which would have had a very disturbing effect. A green filter was used to heighten the contrast.

Plate 32. THE PICTURESQUE – BY ENEMY ACTION

Chiswick Park was one of the first irregular gardens in Europe, as opposed to formal symmetrical gardens, and it is the most picturesque park in London – though not many Londoners seem to be aware of it – with cedar trees, temples, pavilions, vases, and statues from Hadrian's Villa. The grounds were laid out for Lord Burlington by William Kent and Bridgeman between 1715 and 1736.

This close-up was taken the day after enemy action. To me there seemed much poetry in the scene, particularly in the way in which the branches of the tree appear to droop weeping over the victim.

The photographs in this section were taken with a 9 × 12 cm plate camera, except Plates 12, 13, 25, 26, 27, 28.

PLATES 33—64

33. EDWARD II. GLOUCESTER CATHEDRAL

34. EDWARD III'S SHOES

35. EDWARD III. WESTMINSTER ABBEY

36. ANNE OF BOHEMIA. WESTMINSTER ABBEY

37. RICHARD II. WESTMINSTER ABBEY

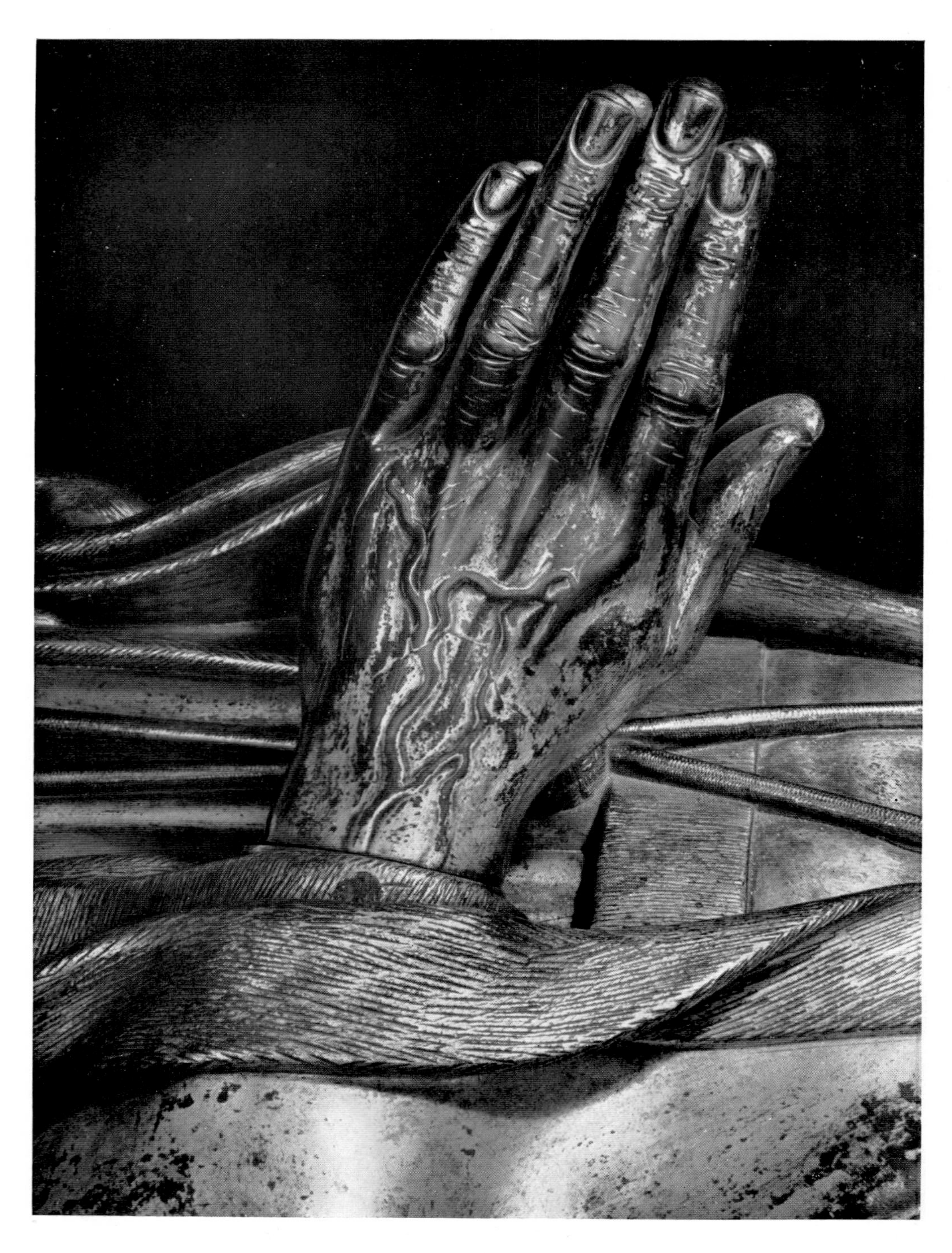

38. HENRY VII'S HANDS

39. HENRY VII. WESTMINSTER ABBEY

40. CHERUB FROM TOMB OF HENRY VII AND ELIZABETH OF YORK. WESTMINSTER ABBEY

41. TOMB OF HENRY, LORD NORRIS. WESTMINSTER ABBEY.

42a. PHILOSOPHER OR PROPHET. HENRY VII'S CHAPEL, WESTMINSTER ABBEY

42b. ST BARBARA. HENRY VII'S CHAPEL, WESTMINSTER ABBEY

43. JOHN ERNST GRABE. POETS' CORNER, WESTMINSTER ABBEY

44. THOMAS THYNNE. WESTMINSTER ABBEY

45. MRS MARY BROCAS, ST MARGARET'S, WESTMINSTER

46a. RELIEF ON MONUMENT TO BISHOP WILCOCKS. WESTMINSTER ABBEY

46b. SIR CLOUDESLEY SHOVELL. WESTMINSTER ABBEY

47. MEMORIAL TO JOHN CHURCHILL.
ST MARGARET'S, WESTMINSTER

48. WOODCARVING IN TRINITY COLLEGE CHAPEL, OXFORD

49. ANGEL, ST MARY'S, HAREFIELD

50. WILLIAM CONGREVE, WESTMINSTER ABBEY

51. DETAIL FROM CHINESE PAVILION, SANSSOUCI

52. MONUMENT TO SIR ISAAC NEWTON, WESTMINSTER ABBEY

53. SIR ISAAC NEWTON, MONUMENT DETAIL NO. 1

54a. NEWTON, MONUMENT DETAIL NO. 2.
THE CHERUBS

54b. NEWTON, MONUMENT DETAIL NO. 3.
THE MASSIVE FOOT OF THE SARCOPHAGUS

57. DETAIL FROM MONUMENT TO JAMES THOMPSON. WESTMINSTER ABBEY

58. GEORGE FREDERICK HANDEL, WESTMINSTER ABBEY

59. DR SAMUEL JOHNSON, WESTMINSTER ABBEY

60*a*

60b

60a. & 60b. WILLIAM SHAKESPEARE, WESTMINSTER ABBEY.
A DEMONSTRATION IN LIGHTING EFFECT

61. MASK FROM MONUMENT TO SAMUEL BUTLER, WESTMINSTER ABBEY

62. DEATH, FROM MONUMENT TO LADY ELIZABETH NIGHTINGALE. WESTMINSTER ABBEY

63. SLAVE, DETAIL FROM MONUMENT TO CHARLES JAMES FOX. WESTMINSTER ABBEY

64. HORATIO, LORD NELSON. ST PAUL'S CATHEDRAL

NOTES TO THE PLATES ON SCULPTURE

WESTMINSTER ABBEY

Westminster Abbey has been called the British Valhalla in the nineteenth century, and the National Shrine in the twentieth. The historic associations which are so closely interwoven in its fabric draw to the Abbey every year thousands of visitors who aimlessly wander around, lost in the spaciousness and gloom of the interior and bewildered by the profusion of monuments to famous and insignificant people alike. For though the Abbey is the last resting place of many who were great in their achievements, more often than not their memory is perpetuated only by a monument or epitaph and they are buried elsewhere. There are also a great many monuments to insignificant people, for up to the end of the 'seventies of the last century, the erection of a monument in the Abbey depended on the right of birth or on payment of a large fee to the Dean and Chapter, and 'the best sites were reserved for those who could pay best for them, while a nook was all that could be conceded to men of imperishable fame'. The power of helping obscure friends to fame by purchase prevailed to a large degree, and in comparison with the sumptuous monuments to the memory of unknown persons, those erected in memory of the great English poets sometimes appear mean. Addison caustically commented on this in *The Spectator*: 'In the poetical quarter I found there were poets who had no monuments, and monuments which had no poets'. Byron was, for instance, denied a place in the Abbey on moral grounds, and neither Keats nor Shelley is remembered by as much as a tablet. On the other hand, the only qualification which procured a monument to one John Phillips seems to have been a poem on the qualities of cider, and a certain Thomas Smith is only remembered for the curious inscription on the tablet: 'Who through ye spotted vaile of the smallpox rendered a pure and unspotted soul to God'.

ROYAL EFFIGIES

Four years ago the public had for the first time an opportunity to appreciate the Royal effigies and other sculpture from Westminster Abbey. I refer to the memorable display at the Victoria and Albert Museum in the winter of 1945-6.

The occasion for this exhibition arose when the effigies were brought back to London from their war-time place of safety. In the Abbey they are so inaccessibly placed that they cannot be closely inspected. For this reason they had never been photographed before.

By no means all the Kings and Queens of England are buried in Westminster Abbey, and of those who are, only a comparatively small number have an effigy. The earliest effigies are those of Henry III and his daughter-in-law, Eleanor of Castile, the first wife of Edward I. There are also effigies of the following kings and queens: – Edward III and Philippa of Hainault, Richard II and his first wife Anne of Bohemia, the headless oak figure of Henry V (the silver head was stolen and melted down in Henry VIII's reign), Henry VII and Elizabeth of York.

All the effigies, with the exception of Philippa of Hainault's marble figure, which was not evacuated, were photographed at their place of safety in the country, where they were lying in a row on the parquet floor of a ballroom. It was evident that before I could start work the effigies would have to be moved apart and a background cloth introduced, for the parquet design had an extremely disturbing effect. This was easier said than done, for three workmen were required to move the effigies.

The ease of access afforded an opportunity unlikely to recur, and so a great many detail photographs were taken of heads, hands, feet, animals supporting the feet, folds of garments, the delicate patterns of the Royal badges punched upon the bronze, etc.

Front and three-quarter views were taken of each effigy. As in life portraiture, the three-quarter views proved in practically every case the more interesting. For the full-face view it was necessary to stand on the effigy itself.

Lighting consisted of two 500-watt floodlights, one held by an assistant behind and slightly above the head of the effigy, the other placed in a frontal position to render translucent the shadows thus cast, and at the same time to give greater plasticity to the head, which is considerably more difficult to achieve in the case of a recumbent figure than in an erect one.

Bronze figures call for very soft negatives: in order to obtain good modulation and highlights which are not 'clogged', comparatively long exposures must be given. Backed negative material is absolutely essential to avoid halation from reflection. The main difficulty I had to contend with was the patchiness of the bronze, due to oxidization: the greatest amount of light often came in direct juxtaposition to a dark patch. Before being returned to the Abbey the figures were cleaned and re-gilded.

Plate 33. EDWARD II, reigned 1307-27. *Gloucester Cathedral*

The tomb was built about 1330 by Edward III in memory of his murdered father. The magnificence of the canopy with its crocketed ogee arches and pinnacles is at once apparent to any visitor to Gloucester Cathedral, but the alabaster effigy is normally only visible in profile. Intent upon obtaining a full-face view, I asked the Dean's permission to squeeze myself inside the canopy. My request was readily granted, and thus the figure, one of the most exquisite works of English medieval sculpture, was photographed for the first time.

Lighting was a major problem. One floodlight was placed in the small space behind the King's head, between the tomb and the pillar. The other lamp was placed at the very opposite end of the tomb to counteract the heavy shadows thus caused. Standing across the figure with legs apart I allowed the beam of light to pass between them. With the wide-angle lens I was *just* able to get both the angels which support the King's head, on the ground glass. When it came to the actual exposure, however, I found that I could not insert the dark-slide into the camera, owing to the narrowness of the canopy. It occurred to me then to ascertain the exact position of the camera by measuring the distance from the lens to two given points downwards and sideways. Having done so I tilted the camera up into the horizontal position, put the dark-slide in, and then tilted it down again to the exact angle according to my measurements, which were – *mirabile dictu* – correct and nothing was cut off.

In conclusion I wish to explain that I am not responsible for the King's broken nose nor for his squinting eyes, and that the deep facial scars were not caused by my tripod. It seems that one other person saw the King as I did. He was a naughty little boy, the son of the organist, who about 1725 scratched his initials 'I.H.' on the King's eyes.

Plate 34. EDWARD III's SHOES. *Westminster Abbey*

The light had to be so placed as to throw sharply into relief the long pointed Gothic shoes, and to accentuate the leaf pattern punched into the metal.

Plate 35. EDWARD III, reigned 1327-77. *Westminster Abbey*

The effigy is probably by John Orchard. The saint-like face cannot be taken as a portrait, but is an idealised representation, rather unsuitable for a soldier king. Originally a crown was set upon the king's head and the mark where it was is clearly visible.

Plate 36. ANNE OF BOHEMIA, RICHARD II's FIRST WIFE, b. 1366 d. 1394 *Westminster Abbey*

Plate 37. RICHARD II, reigned 1377-1399. *Westminster Abbey*

Richard of Bordeaux was the only reigning sovereign to be married at Westminster Abbey. His wife, Anne of Bohemia, was a daughter of the Emperor Charles IV.

After the death of his queen in 1394 the king ordered effigies of both her and himself from Nicholas Broker and Godfrey Prest, two London coppersmiths. Richard, who was most devoted to Anne, ordered that the figures, which are intended to be portraits, should have their right hands clasped together; but fate willed otherwise – their arms were stolen later, and so were their jewelled crowns.

Plate 38. HENRY VII's HANDS. *Westminster Abbey*

The correct camera height was of great importance for this photograph: by going lower with the camera the hands would probably have appeared more dramatic through their isolation, but at the same time they would have become less readily understandable in relation to the figure; most important of all, the left hand would have been superimposed on the right one, rendering it completely invisible.

Plate 39. HENRY VII, reigned 1485-1509. *Westminster Abbey*

Detail from the monument by Pietro Torrigiani. This is clearly a portrait of the king, who wears a flat topped cap with lappets. His head rests on a cushion; his beautifully modelled hands are folded in prayer.

Plate 40. CHERUB FROM TOMB OF HENRY VII AND ELIZABETH OF YORK. *Westminster Abbey*

There are four cherubs, one at each corner of the tomb designed by Pietro Torrigiani about 1510.

The cherubs, like the Royal effigies, were lying on a parquet floor. In order to regain the effect they have *in situ* I had them taken out of doors and placed in a sitting position at a corner of the building, supported by a table. The photograph was taken in sunlight.

Plate 41. TOMB OF HENRY, LORD NORRIS, d. 1601. *Westminster Abbey. Detail*

Lord and Lady Norris were held in high esteem by Queen Elizabeth, who sent him to France as Ambassador and called his wife her 'own dear Crow'.

The illustration shows only one of a number of detail photographs of the effigies and canopy of this grand Elizabethan monument, erected in 1603, probably by Epiphanius Evesham. Around the parents kneel their six sons, three on each side of the tomb. The features are presumably likenesses.

St Andrew's Chapel, in which the monument stands, was completely dark at the time the photographs were taken, due to the fact that the windows were boarded up. The main problem was to carve the figures out of the darkness in such a way as to avoid undue prominence being given to the jumble of mainly bad nineteenth century sculpture surrounding it.

Plate 42a. PHILOSOPHER OR PROPHET. *Henry VII's Chapel, Westminster Abbey*

Plate 42b. ST BARBARA. *Henry VII's Chapel, Westminster Abbey*

The figures are about three feet high, of whitewashed stone, and stand on pedestals in richly carved niches round the triforium of Henry VII's Chapel. Originally there were 107 figures, of which 95 remain. They date from about 1500 and are from the hands of a number of sculptors and master-masons, and therefore of varying merit. Worked in the late Gothic manner, they stand in strong contrast to Torrigiani's magnificent Renaissance tomb and figures of almost the same date. Inaccessible because of their lofty position in the Chapel, they afforded close study at the exhibition in the Victoria and Albert Museum, where I photographed a great many of them for the Society of Antiquaries. As far as possible I strove to maintain the feeling of looking up to the figures by taking a low camera angle, in this way also avoiding the ugly join between vertical and horizontal background, so often seen cutting through figures in photographs. As the blue mottled exhibition walls would have proved a disturbing factor in the photographs I decided to use a plain linen background, which was stretched on a large piece of plywood and moved behind each figure, which had for this reason to be brought forward from the wall. Though the figures were well lit by the existing fluorescent lighting, this proved too soft and shadowless for my purpose and was therefore supplemented for part of the exposure by one additional floodlight which I lifted high above the figures' heads.

Plate 43. John Ernest Grabe, d. 1711. *Poets' Corner, Westminster Abbey*

Grabe was a German orientalist who settled in this country. He sits on his sarcophagus, and as befits a learned professor, is seen studiously writing--apparently up to the last moment before death. (The right hand, holding a quill evidently just in the act of dipping it in the inkpot also provided by the sculptor, must be left to the reader's imagination).

As if already floating heavenwards, this admirer of the Church of England was placed exceedingly high up in the Abbey. It was quite impossible to light the monument from above, but the shadows were so arranged as to give the greatest possible plasticity to the figure and to detach it from the white wall. Four planes are clearly discernible: the knees, the hand holding the book, the main body, and the wall. The camera was placed at such a height as to allow a close-up, but at the same time retaining the effect of looking up to the monument which is implicit in the design of the sculptor, Francis Bird.

Plate 44. Thomas Thynne, d. 1682. *Westminster Abbey*

Thomas Thynne, one of the richest men in England, married the young widow of the Earl of Ogle and heiress of the Earl of Northumberland. A year after his marriage Thynne was murdered in his coach in the Haymarket by three men who were friends of Count Königsmarck, who designed to marry the rich widow. However, Count Königsmarck and the three assassins were caught and tried, and the latter were hanged, but the Count was acquitted in accordance with the known wish of the King. The widow married – not the Count, but the Duke of Somerset – being thus three times married before she was sixteen years old. A bas-relief beneath Thynne's reclining figure depicts the scene of the murder.

Thynne looks heavenward and his expression seems to cry for mercy. I arranged my lights high above his head, thereby heightening the dramatic effect and intensifying the baroque feeling of the monument by Thomas Quellin.

The *Architectural Review* wrote of this photograph: 'The bold and sweeping shadows throw into prominence what is expressive. The photographer may lose a little too much of the detail in the hair, but then the Baroque never quibbled over detail. It is the larger facts that matter, and they come out to a degree which would no doubt enrapture Quellinus if he could come back to see them.'

Plate 45. MRS MARY BROCAS, d. 1654. *St Margaret's, Westminster*

Though this monument by Joshua Marshall is not particularly important, it has been included because it illustrates an interesting photographic point. After having taken a frontal view my task seemed finished, but on going to the side of the monument to put the dark-slide back into the case, I was suddenly struck by the beautiful effect which the lights gave to the face, now seen in profile, and with practically no alteration in the lighting I obtained this detail photograph, which I have often exhibited under the title *Portrait in Stone*. The head has exceptionally high plastic qualities and almost seems alive. The shadow of the curved niche throws the profile splendidly into relief, while the deep shadow at the back of the head hides an ungainly feature – its attachment to the wall. The moral of this is that one should study a monument from all sides if one wishes to discover new pleasures or obtain unusual photographs.

Plate 46a. RELIEF ON MONUMENT TO BISHOP WILCOCKS, d. 1756. *Westminster Abbey*

As a change from the monuments in Westminster Abbey, here is Westminster Abbey on a monument.

The western towers were completed by Nicholas Hawksmoor during the twenty-five years that Bishop Wilcocks was Dean of Westminster. He desired this fact to be commemorated on his monument, which was erected five years after his death. The delightful rococo relief is by Sir Henry Cheere, who was a pupil of Scheemakers and became a brilliant exponent of the Rococo in English sculpture.

Plate 46b. SIR CLOUDESLEY SHOVELL, d. 1707. *Westminster Abbey*

The monument to Sir Cloudesley Shovell, the Commander of the Fleet, was commissioned from Grinling Gibbons by Queen Anne. In 1707 the most violent storm ever known in British waters wrecked part of the fleet, including the flagship, and the Admiral was washed ashore on the Scilly Isles. Thirty years later, a fisherwoman confessed on her deathbed that she had found him unconscious and put an end to his life for the sake of obtaining his valuable ring.

The famous woodcarver was also a sculptor, and this is one of the few monuments by him in the Abbey. The Admiral is represented wearing a Roman toga and a wig – an incongruous but quite common mixture of costume in statues at that time.

Plate 47. MEMORIAL TO JOHN CHURCHILL, d. 1715. *St Margaret's, Westminster*

Like the Abbey, St Margaret's, Westminster (which has been for over three centuries the official church of the House of Commons) is packed to capacity with monuments.

This gay memorial tablet would have lost a good deal of its effect if photographed frontally. The view chosen brings out incomparably better its baroque character, which forms an amusing contrast to the solemnity of the church expressed by the Gothic windows.

Mrs Esdaile mentions as probable sculptor John Churchill's brother Robert.

Plate 48. WOODCARVING IN TRINITY COLLEGE CHAPEL, OXFORD

The limewood carving round the High Altar is generally regarded as Grinling Gibbons' masterpiece. Grinling Gibbons, who came originally from Holland, was the most famous of the craftsmen who collaborated with Wren. This detail, from the left-hand side of the High Altar, is a good example of Grinling Gibbon's exuberance in woodcarving. Apart from his usual flowers, fruit and leaves, there are some open pea pods.

Plate 49. ANGEL. *St Mary's, Harefield*

This little country church, which has for centuries been connected with the Newdigate family, is rich in monuments, which crowd the walls. The angel of which this close-up was taken, kneels to the right of the altar, and is a late seventeenth century woodcarving, possibly Flemish.

The light from the east window falls only on the right side of the angel's face: to give an even effect and good modelling it had to be supplemented by one floodlight held above the head. The play of light from both sides will nearly always achieve the greatest roundness in sculpture. Every feature stands out plastically from its surroundings by the play of light against dark and dark against light.

Plate 50. WILLIAM CONGREVE, d. 1729. *Westminster Abbey*

Congreve was considered by his contemporaries to be the leading dramatist of the age: Dryden even compared him to Shakespeare. His funeral was a very pompous ceremony. No less a person than the Prime Minister was one of the pall-bearers.

The monument is arranged within the Gothic arcading of the south aisle. The medallion-like setting of Congreve's portrait, sculptured by Francis Bird after the Kit Kat portrait by Kneller, and surrounded by masks, has great charm and is unique in the Abbey.

Plate 51. DETAIL FROM CHINESE PAVILION, *Sanssouci*

The Tea House in the Park of Sanssouci was built for Frederick the Great between 1754-7, following the fashion of the time for *chinoiserie*.

The gilded bronze figure was photographed in daylight during a visit to Potsdam in 1936. Though essentially a detail photograph, care was taken not to isolate the figure too much, the arm and hand of the seated cavalier indicating at whom the charming lady is looking.

Plate 52. MONUMENT TO SIR ISAAC NEWTON, d. 1727. *Westminster Abbey*

The monument was erected, four years after the great scientist's death, in the most prominent position in the nave, against the rood screen (the outer stonework is neo-Gothic and was erected in 1831).

The monument was designed by William Kent and sculptured by John Michael Rysbrack, who came from Antwerp, settled in England, and became one of the most famous sculptors of his day.

Newton leans on the four folios which brought him fame: *Divinity*, *Chronology*, *Optics* and *Philosophiæ Naturalis Principia Mathematica*. His left hand points to two cherubs reciting his achievements from a scroll. Above the group is the celestial globe with the constellations, and reclining on it an allegorical figure representing Astronomy. The bas-relief on the sarcophagus symbolises Newton's theory of gravitation, his researches on light, colour, and other natural phenomena.

After the Royal effigies, the Newton monument is probably the most important in the Abbey, and afforded scope for a number of detail photographs. It has therefore been chosen to explain my working methods more clearly. Whereas in other plates I was only able to give one close-up, usually much more interesting pictorially than the whole monument, the subjoined plates show the whole Newton monument and all the details I took, with the exception of the bas-relief on the sarcophagus which is not particularly attractive, and obscure in meaning.

Plate 53. DETAIL No. 1. SIR ISAAC NEWTON

'A masterpiece of baroque portraiture, heroic, yet eloquent and human', wrote Sir Kenneth Clark of this head.

Plate 54a. DETAIL No. 2. THE CHERUBS

The cherubs, a prominent feature of baroque and rococo art, form a charming group in themselves, and from the viewpoint from which they were taken are, I think, well related to the whole monument by the inclusion of Newton's left hand and part of the celestial globe.

Plate 54b. DETAIL No. 3. THE MASSIVE FOOT OF THE SARCOPHAGUS

Plate 55. DETAIL No. 4. THE CELESTIAL GLOBE

It will be obvious to the reader, as it was to me at the time, that the effect of this picture would be spoiled if the shadow of the globe were running upwards instead of downwards. I was greatly relieved when my assistant volunteered to climb with the floodlight on top of 'Astronomy'. The bold design was thus intentionally dramatised, the rotundity of the globe with its delicate relief work accentuated, and this no doubt added greatly to the plasticity of the sculpture. Light alone, however, did not bring out the Zodiacal signs: the globe had first to be cleaned of a thick layer of dust.

Plate 56. JOHN, SECOND DUKE OF ARGYLL, d. 1743. *Westminster Abbey*

This famous orator and soldier lies buried in Henry VII's Chapel. He was mainly instrumental in bringing about the Union of England and Scotland in 1707.

The Duke's elaborate monument is placed in the Poets' Corner, silhouetted against the daylight. Like most of the baroque monuments in the Abbey, the pictorial possibilities of which depend entirely upon good lighting effects, it is placed in the worst possible position – enough to break the heart of the sculptor, Roubiliac. The head, which is some fifteen feet from the Abbey floor, gives us a glimpse of the dramatic possibilities inherent in his work.

Like the other two leading baroque sculptors in England – Rysbrack and Scheemakers – Roubiliac came from the Continent, but whereas they were Flemish, he came from France.

Plate 57. DETAIL FROM MONUMENT TO JAMES THOMPSON, d. 1748.
Westminster Abbey

The monument to the author of *The Seasons* was erected only in 1762, from a design by Robert Adam, sculptured by the Dane, Michael Spang. The plate shows the bas-relief round the pedestal, depicting the seasons, to which a cherub draws the beholder's attention.

Some difficulty was experienced in giving depth to the relief, owing to the impossibility of getting close to it, and also to its pronounced curvature. The light was therefore placed below the pedestal, where it could be brought closer to the relief than in any other position.

Plate 58. GEORGE FREDERICK HANDEL, d. 1759. *Westminster Abbey*

The monument to the great composer was erected in 1762 and is by Roubiliac, who made his fame in London with another statue of Handel for Vauxhall Gardens in 1738.

Having published a close-up of the figure in my book *New Photo Vision*, I have preferred this time to illustrate the whole monument, in its setting of Early English arcading, which offers a better glimpse of its theatrical air than the close-up. We imagine Handel here as the bustling director of one of his operas rather than as the composer of the great oratorio *Messiah*, from which a few bars of the favourite aria 'I know that my Redeemer liveth' are recorded on the marble music sheets.

Roubiliac knew Handel well and we can assume that the life-size figure is a likeness.

This is another of the monuments which are placed exceedingly high up and the wealth of detail revealed by my floodlights caused the late Dean Labillière, who saw me at work, to remark that he would like to install a floodlighting system in the Abbey to show the public the splendour of some of the more important monuments which, owing to their deplorable position and the dim lighting conditions prevailing, could not give a proper impression to the visitor.

Plate 59. DR SAMUEL JOHNSON, d.1784. *Westminster Abbey*

The front view of Nollekens' bust of the famous lexicographer is not particularly attractive because of the Doctor's fat flabby face. The profile is certainly more flattering, and the play of light and shade gives a lifelike appearance to the bust.

Plates 60a and 60b. WILLIAM SHAKESPEARE, d.1616. *Westminster Abbey*

'What needs my Shakespeare for his honour'd bones,
The labour of an age in pilèd stones!'

Milton's lines seem prophetically applicable to this monument in the Abbey, which was erected by public subscription one hundred and twenty-four years after Shakespeare's death. It was designed by William Kent and sculptured by Scheemakers, a Flemish artist who, with Rysbrack and Roubiliac, forms the triad of great baroque sculptors in England.

I photographed the poet's head twice, and give both versions here because they illustrate better than words what a tremendous difference lighting can make to sculpture. Just as the character of a landscape will appear entirely different in morning and evening light, so also the direction of artificial light will produce entirely different pictures. My first choice was to light up the head from below, hoping thus to impart to the figure some emotional quality, something of the actor and poet, which finds so little expression in the monument. This unorthodox lighting was not liked by the Warburg Institute, and I was asked to take another photograph, lighting the head in the usual manner. This I did, but my preference is for the first picture. The second version stresses too much the aspect of Shakespeare the gallant courtier; it is an expressionless face.

Plate 61. MASK FROM MONUMENT TO SAMUEL BUTLER, d. 1680. *Westminster Abbey*

Samuel Butler is buried at St Paul's, Covent Garden, because there was no money to pay for a grave in the Abbey. The monument was erected in 1721 by the Lord Mayor, John Barber, 'in order that he who had been denied almost everything in life might not in death be denied a tomb'. This epitaph inspired Pope to these spiteful lines:

' But whence this Barber? that a name so mean
Should, joined with Butler's, on a tomb be seen'.

The sculptor of the mask is unknown, but its beauty is so great that I included it rather than the bust of Butler himself. Perhaps this picture may inspire other photographers to pay more attention to ornaments. When I commented once on the absence of such detail photographs in the portfolios of another photographer, he exclaimed with surprise: 'But they are *only* ornaments!' meaning that as such, they were not worth his attention.

Plate 62. DEATH, FROM MONUMENT TO LADY ELIZABETH NIGHTINGALE d. 1731. *Westminster Abbey*

Another Roubiliac monument, erected in 1761 and placed against a window in the Chapel of St Michael. With gruesome realism Death is seen stepping out of the tomb chamber, clutching with his left hand at the garment of Lady Elizabeth Nightingale and aiming his spear at her with his right hand. According to Mrs Esdaile, the sculptor is expressing an historic fact recorded by local tradition, for Lady Elizabeth, we are told, was struck by lightning – hence the suddenness of Death's attack. At the time of its erection the figure of Death caused a great outcry, but in 1943 the *Architectural Review* came forward with a re-valuation of the monument: 'In any other country such a *chef d'œuvre* would be exhibited as part of the unchallengeable national heritage.'

I photographed Death slightly from the side (in relation to the whole monument) in order to get the maximum out of the dramatic force expressed in the curve of the skeleton and the powerful swing back of the right arm, while at the same time bringing into prominence the ribs, spine and pelvis, which would have been obscured in a frontal view.

Plate 63. SLAVE, DETAIL FROM MONUMENT TO CHARLES JAMES FOX, d. 1806 *Westminster Abbey*

Charles James Fox's monument by Sir Richard Westmacott is an interesting example of nineteenth century sculpture in Westminster Abbey. The sculptor introduced a negro kneeling at the feet of Charles James Fox to symbolise the gratitude felt by negroes all over the world for his efforts towards the abolition of the Slave Trade, which came about in 1807.

The Hellenised head of the negro is extremely fine. The frontal view of the *monument* shows the negro's head in profile and gives no impression of the magnificent muscle and bone modelling and the deep expression in the eyes; so this detail was taken facing the *figure*.

Plate 64. HORATIO, LORD NELSON, d. 1805. *St Paul's Cathedral*

When towards the end of the eighteenth century the Abbey became overcrowded with monuments and no good sites worthy of national heroes could be found, a new Valhalla had to be thought of, and the obvious choice was St Paul's Cathedral. The Dean and Chapter, who had up to 1794 'preserved a Puritan tradition of iconophobia', suddenly reversed their policy and allowed sculptured monuments to be erected. Colossal sums were spent to commemorate fallen naval and military heroes in huge piles of stone. Apart from the Wellington monument, erected in 1852, the memorials in St Paul's betray some of the worst excesses of monumental art, to which stands in poignant contrast the simple marble slab marking the grave of its architect Sir Christopher Wren. For this reason only one plate, the head of Lord Nelson, has been selected for illustration. (Nelson seems to have hoped for burial at Westminster Abbey, for it is reported that at the Battle of Cape St Vincent he cried: 'Westminster Abbey or glorious victory!')

The monument betrays little of Flaxman's usual Neo-Hellenism. Nelson stands on a pedestal which is adorned by allegorical figures, while Britannia points him out to two naval cadets: it goes without saying that the 'embellishment' would not be complete without the huge British lion which balances the group on the other side of the monument.

The composition is in the south transept and is better lighted than any other monument in the Cathedral. Hampered by the impossibility of lighting the head from above with floodlights, owing to its very great height from the Cathedral floor, I carefully studied for several days the play of sunlight which fell on the figure for only about half an hour each morning, and eventually had everything prepared and took this picture from a tall ladder.

The photographs in this section were taken with a 9 × 12 cm plate camera, except Plate 51, which was taken with a Rolleiflex.